YOU CAN TEACH YOURSELF®

GUITAR CHORDS

S0-BBX-228

You Can Teach Yourself® Guitar Chords presents a new system of learning guitar chords. You will learn a wide variety of guitar chords in all keys and in all positions on up the guitar fingerboard. Guitar chords in this book are classified into five basic zones. By learning each zone carefully and by playing the review studies contained at the end of each zone presentation, you will gain knowledge of chord forms and great technical ability in changing quickly from one chord to another. At the end of the book, an important appendix is included which teaches scale and chord construction and which also presents additional chord forms in each zone.

Visit us on the Web at http://www.melbay.com — E-mail us at email@melbay.com

2

Contents

Guide to Chord Diagrams

THE LEFT HAND
(L. H.)

The Left Hand Position

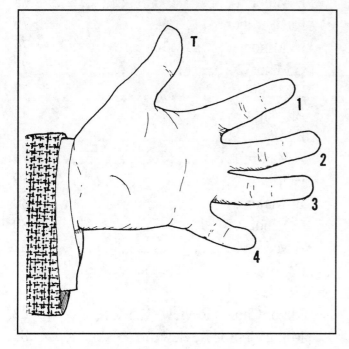

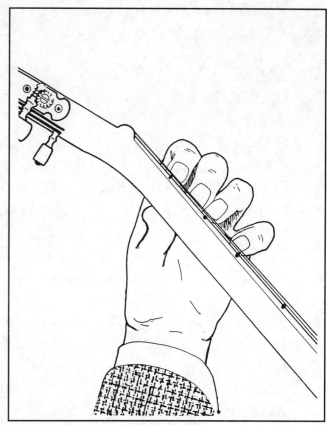

Place your fingers **firmly** on the strings **directly behind the frets**.

STRINGS

BARRE MARKING
**(In this case barre from low G
to high G with 1st Finger)**

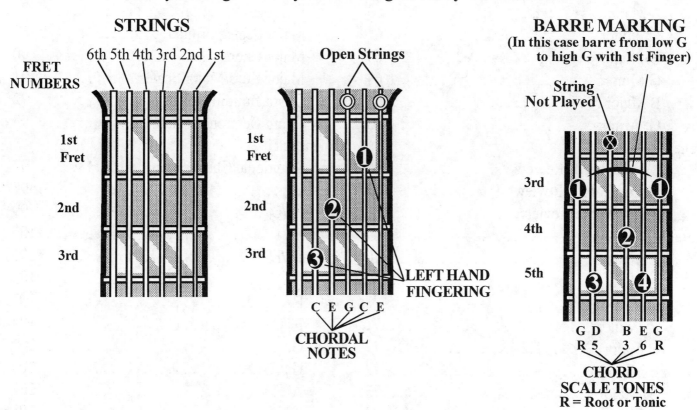

String
Not Played

FRET
NUMBERS

6th 5th 4th 3rd 2nd 1st

Open Strings

1st
Fret

2nd

3rd

1st
Fret

2nd

3rd

3rd

4th

5th

LEFT HAND
FINGERING

C E G C E

CHORDAL
NOTES

G D   B E G
R 5   3 6 R

CHORD
SCALE TONES
R = Root or Tonic

Zone I

In Zone I the 1st Finger of the Left Hand
will always be between the First and Third Frets.

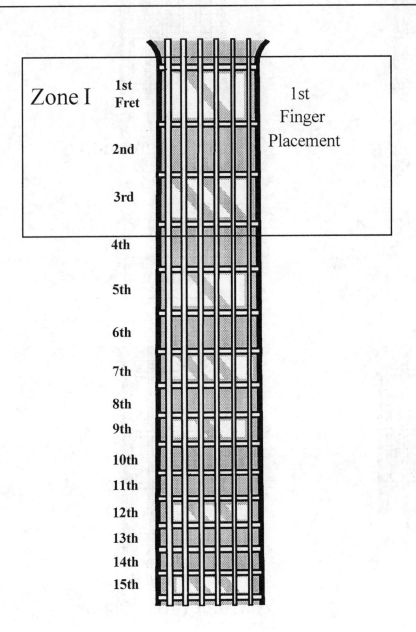

Zone I

| 1st Fret |
| 2nd |
| 3rd |
| 4th |
| 5th |
| 6th |
| 7th |
| 8th |
| 9th |
| 10th |
| 11th |
| 12th |
| 13th |
| 14th |
| 15th |

1st
Finger
Placement

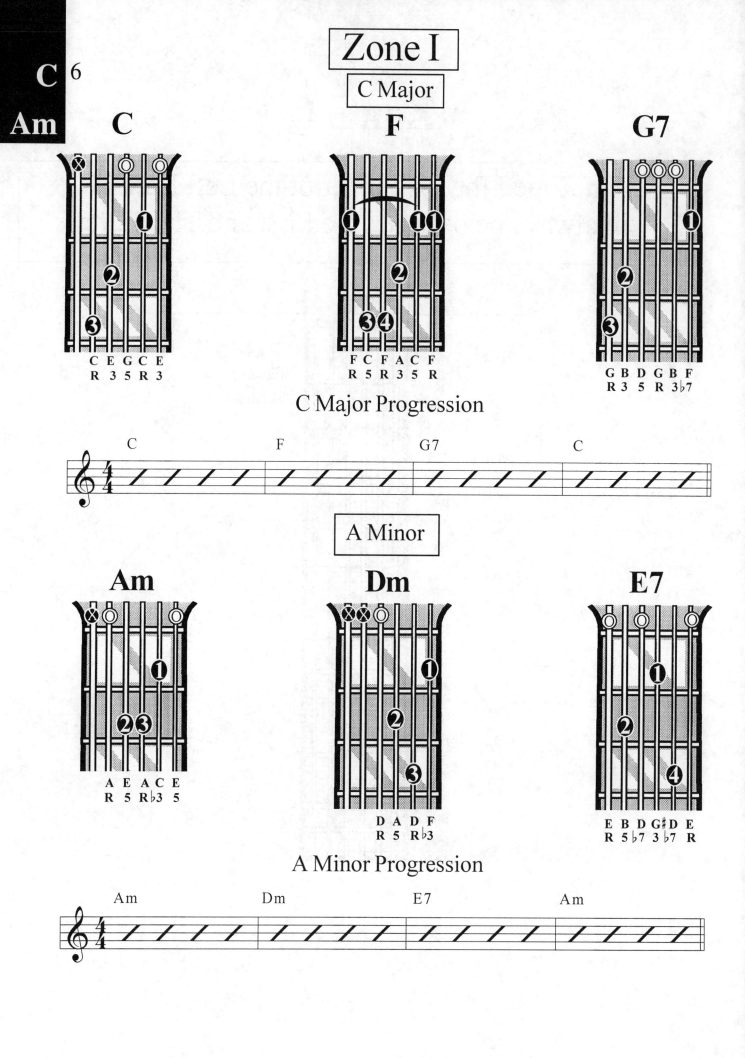

Zone I

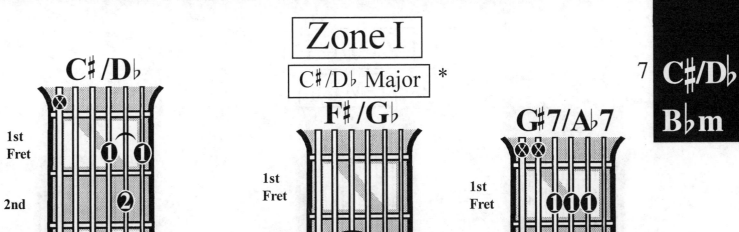

C#/D♭ Major *

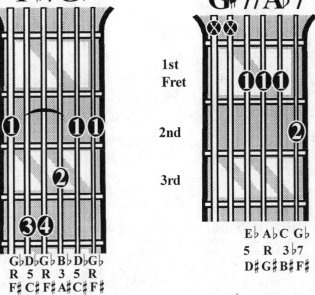

F#/D♭ Major Progression

| D♭ | G♭ | A♭7 | D♭ |

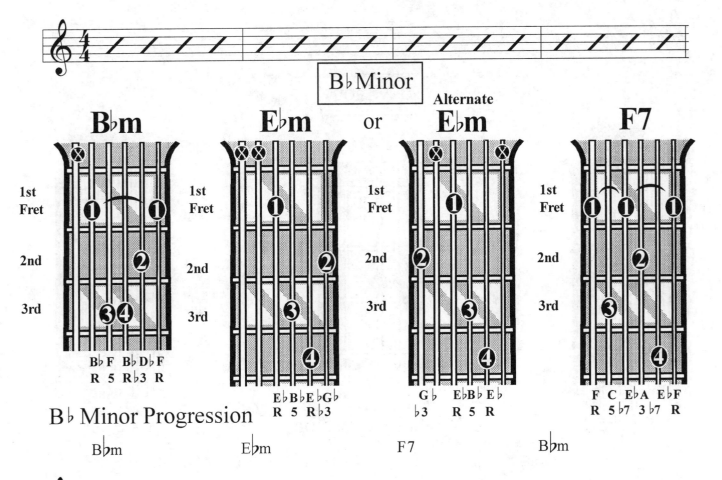

B♭ Minor Progression

| B♭m | E♭m | F7 | B♭m |

* C# and D♭ are called enharmonic keys. The notes sound the same. Thus, D♭ is the same as C#, A♭ is the same as G#, etc.

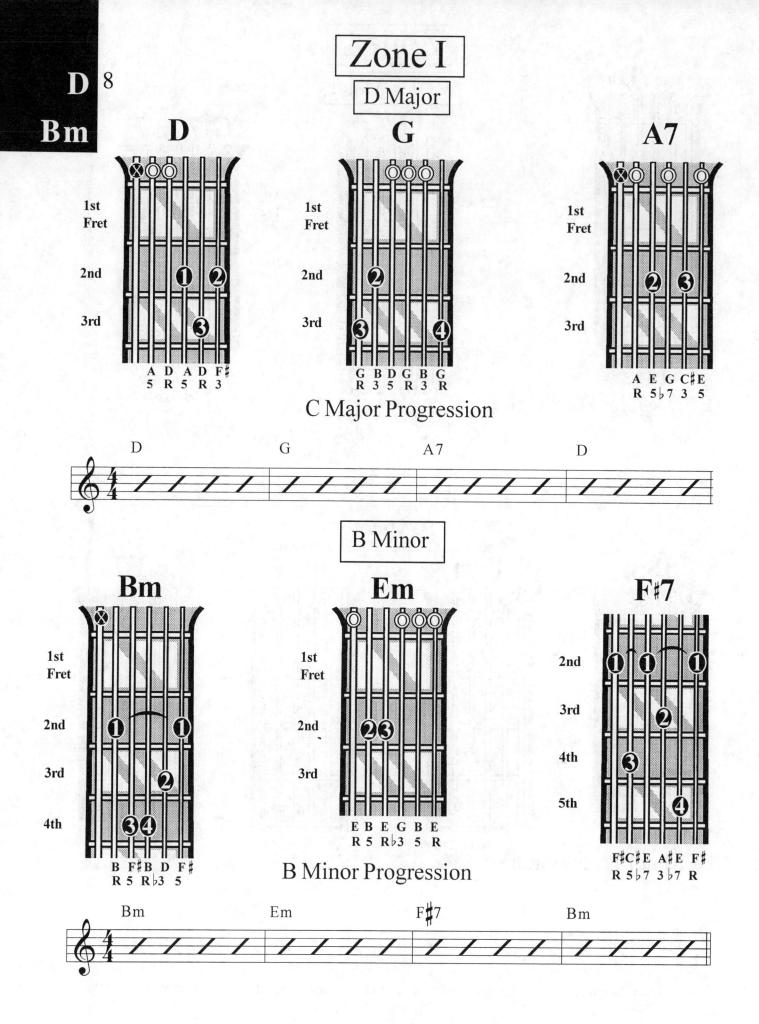

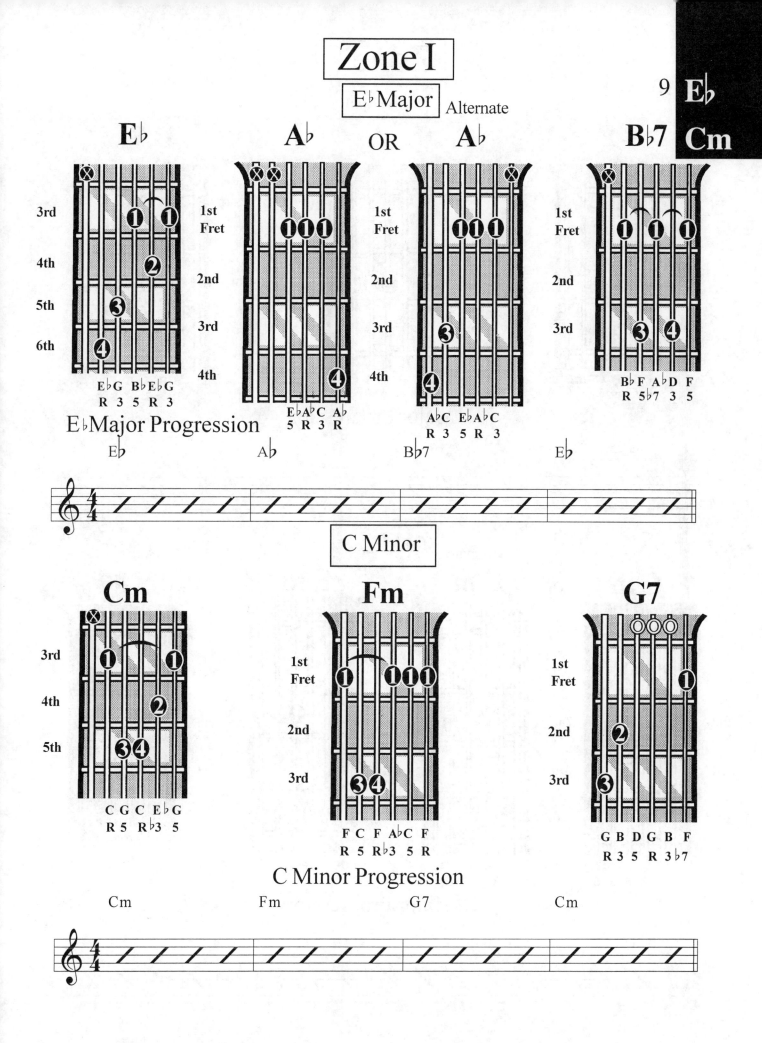

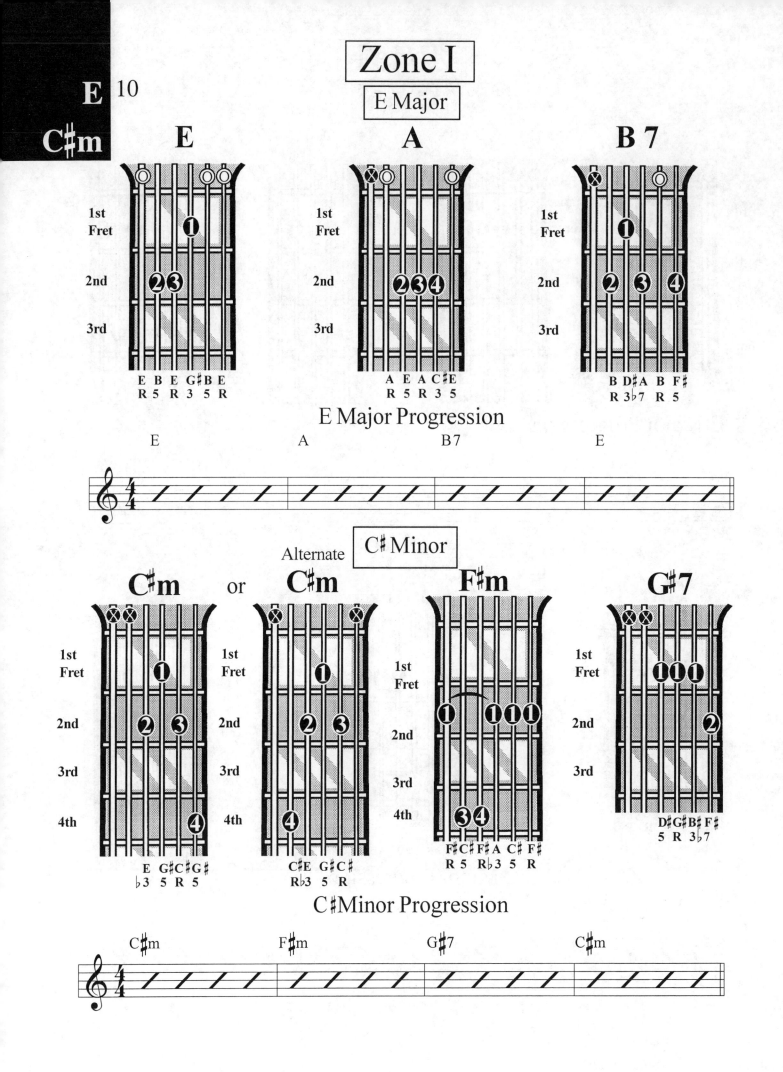

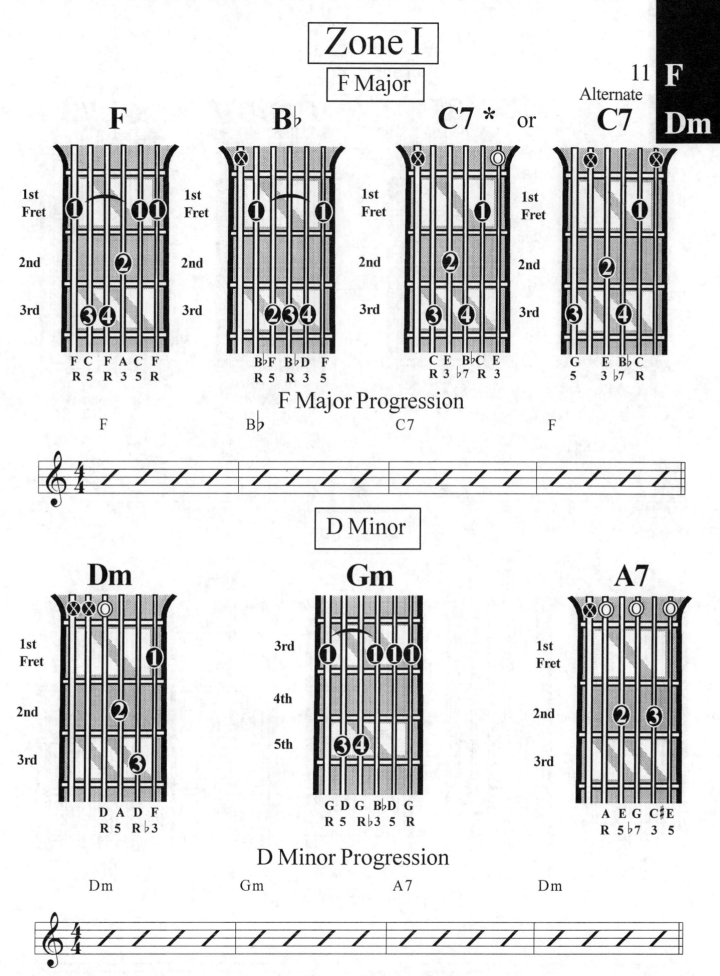

F Major

F   **B♭**   **C7 *** or **C7**   Alternate

F C F A C F
R 5 R 3 5 R

B♭ F B♭ D F
R 5 R 3 5

C E B♭ C E
R 3 ♭7 R 3

G E B♭ C
5 3 ♭7 R

F Major Progression

F   B♭   C7   F

D Minor

Dm   **Gm**   **A7**

D A D F
R 5 R ♭3

G D G B♭ D G
R 5 R ♭3 5 R

A E G C♯ E
R 5 ♭7 3 5

D Minor Progression

Dm   Gm   A7   Dm

* This is a common dominant 7 form. Whenever it occurs in this book, you may also play the alternate form as pictured.

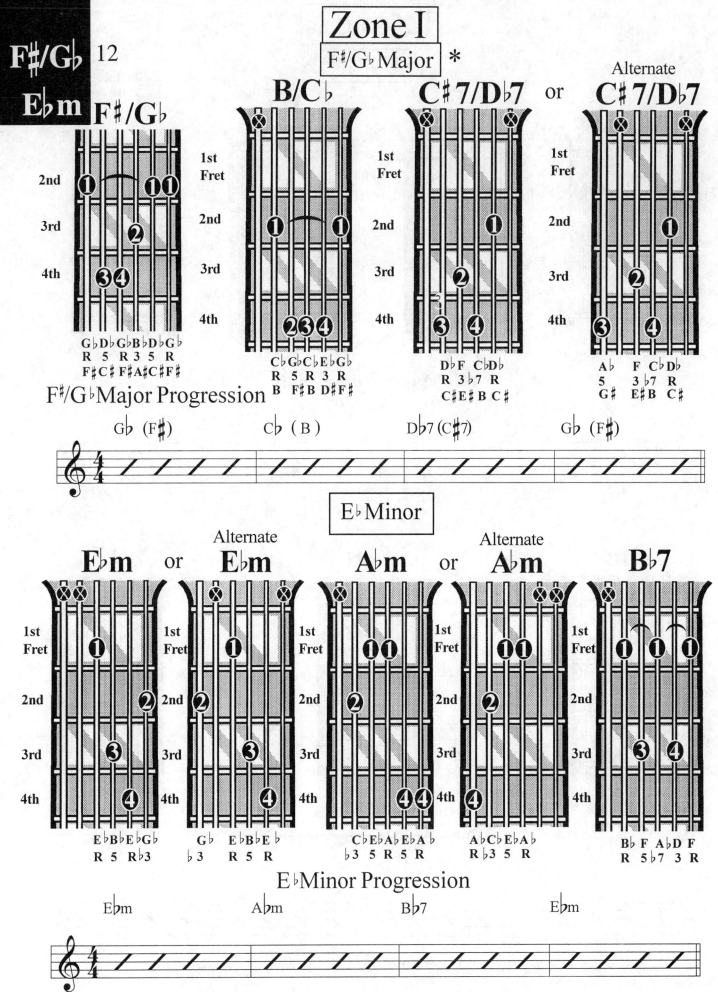

Zone I
F#/Gb Major *

F#/Gb

2nd ① ① ①
3rd ②
4th ③④

GbDbGbBbDbGb
R 5 R 3 5 R
F#C# F#A#C#F#

F#/Gb Major Progression

B/Cb

1st Fret
2nd ① ①
3rd
4th ②③④

CbGbCbEbGb
R 5 R 3 R
B F#B D#F#

C#7/Db7 or

1st Fret
2nd ①
3rd ②
4th ③ ④

DbF CbDb
R 3 b7 R
C#E# B C#

Alternate
C#7/Db7

1st Fret
2nd ①
3rd ②
4th ③ ④

Ab F CbDb
5 3 b7 R
G# E#B C#

Gb (F#)	Cb (B)	Db7 (C#7)	Gb (F#)

𝄞 4/4 / / / / | / / / / | / / / / | / / / /

Eb Minor

Ebm or

1st Fret ①
2nd ②
3rd ③
4th ④

EbBbEbGb
R 5 Rb3

Alternate
Ebm

1st Fret ①
2nd ②
3rd ③
4th ④

Gb EbBbEb
b3 R 5 R

Abm or

1st Fret ① ①
2nd ②
3rd
4th ④④

CbEbAbEbAb
b3 5 R 5 R

Alternate
Abm

1st Fret ① ①
2nd ②
3rd
4th ④

AbCbEbAb
R b3 5 R

Bb7

1st Fret ① ① ①
2nd
3rd ③ ④
4th

Bb F AbD F
R 5 b7 3 R

Eb Minor Progression

Ebm	Abm	Bb7	Ebm

𝄞 4/4 / / / / | / / / / | / / / / | / / / /

* F# and Gb are called enharmonic keys. The notes are the same. Thus Gb is the same note as F#.

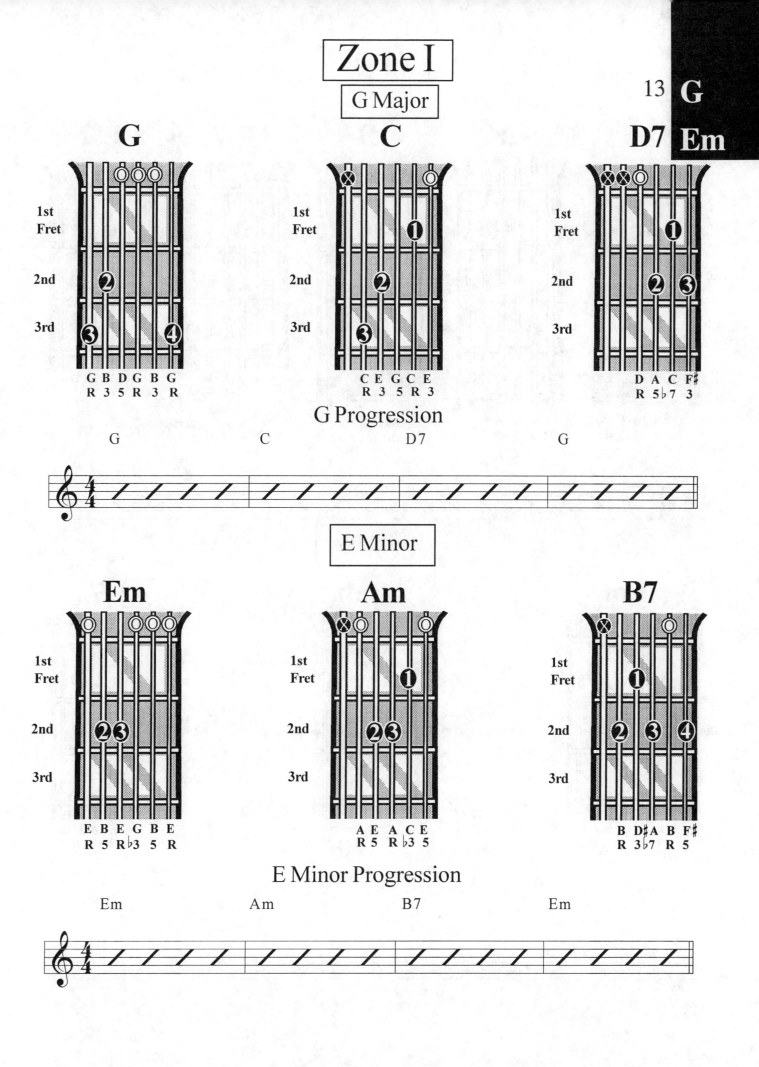

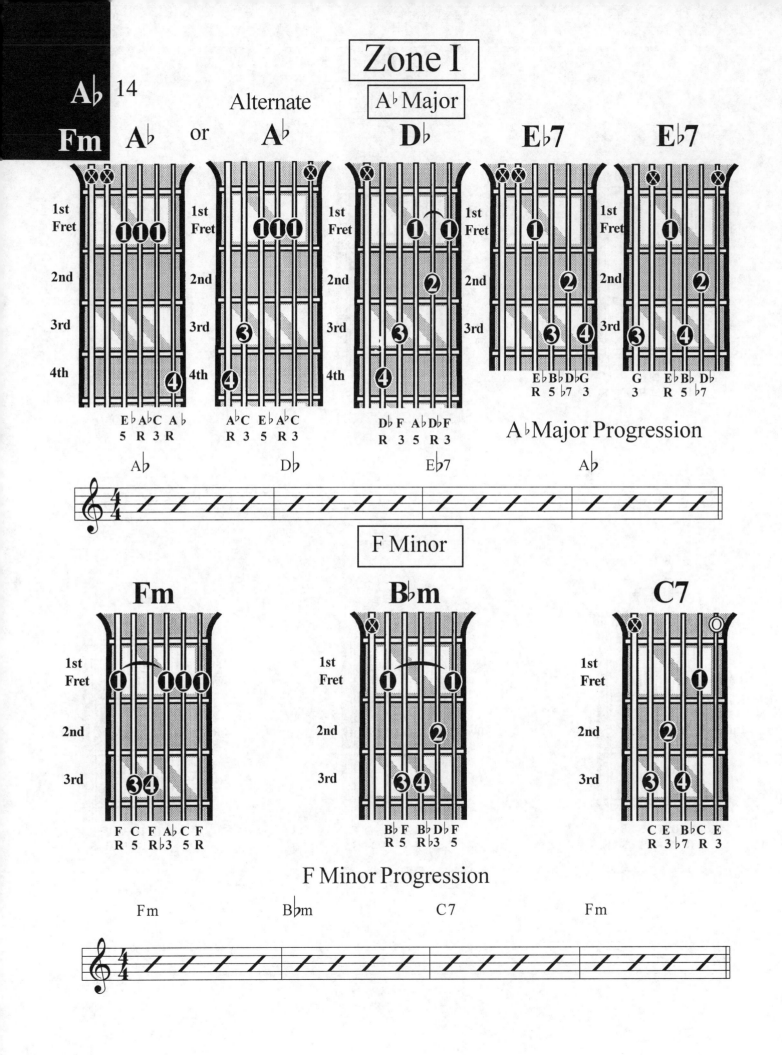

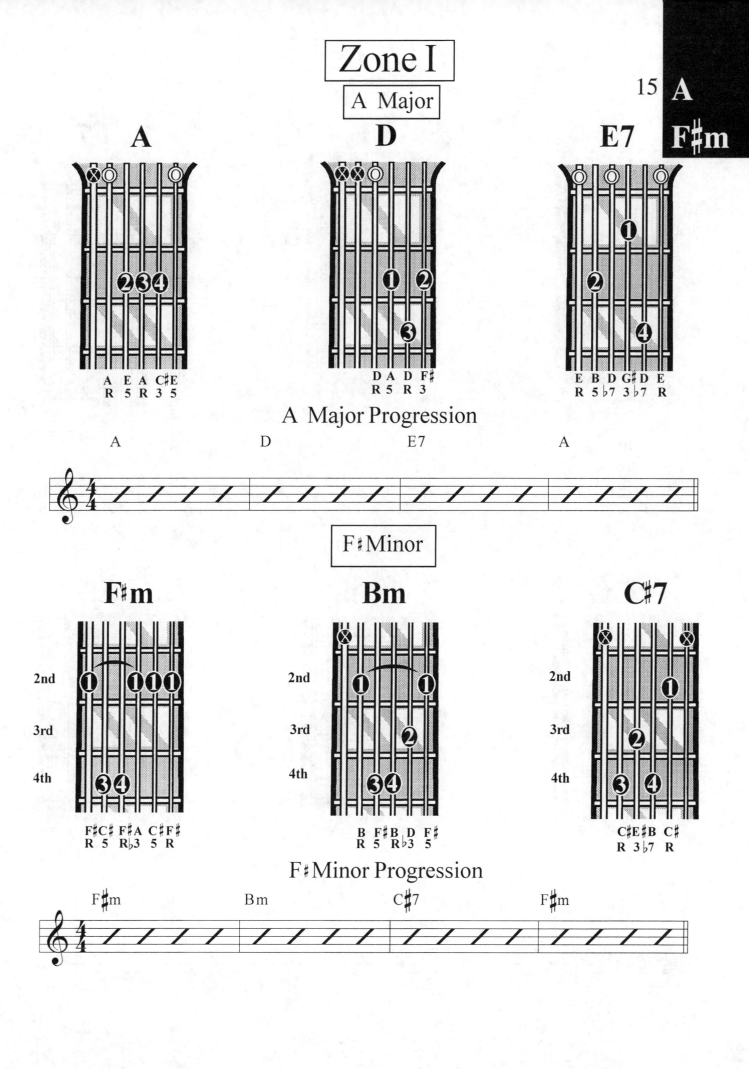

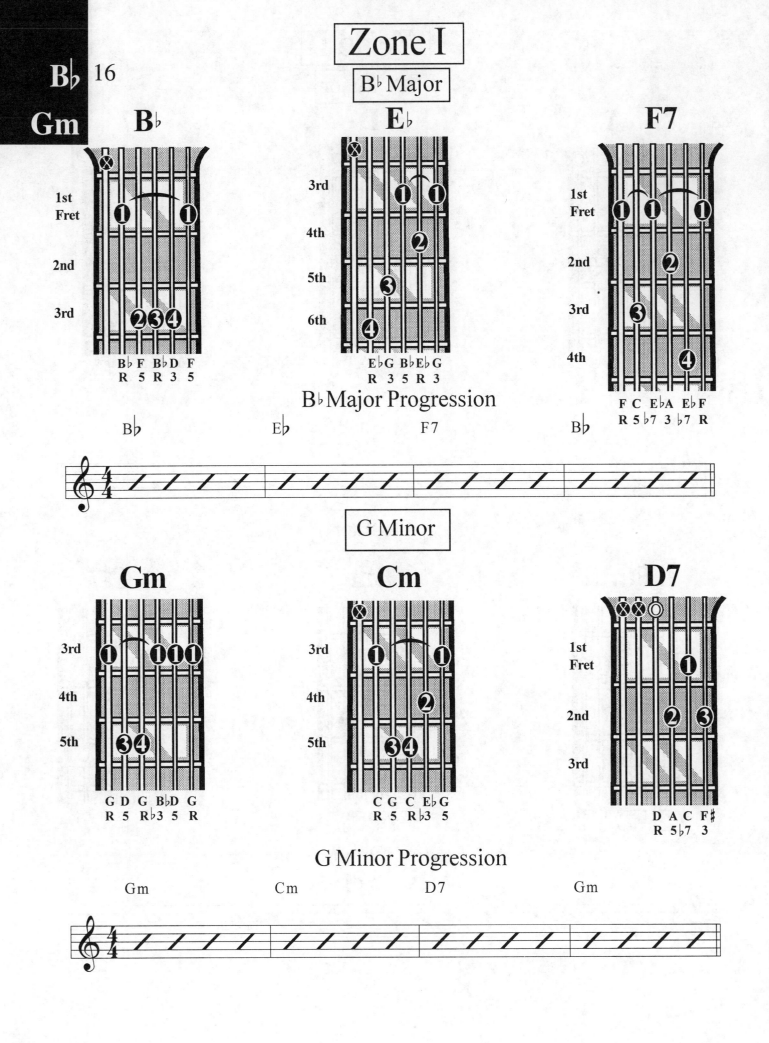

Zone I

B Major

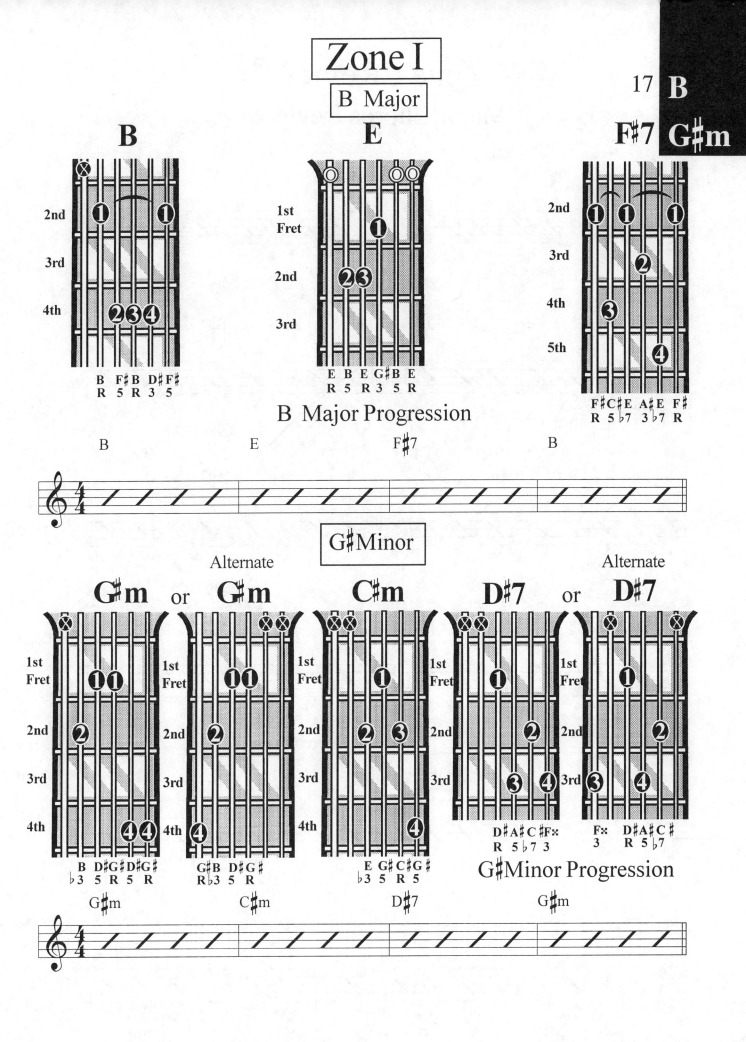

B Major Progression

G♯Minor Progression

Zone I Review
Major Chords Review

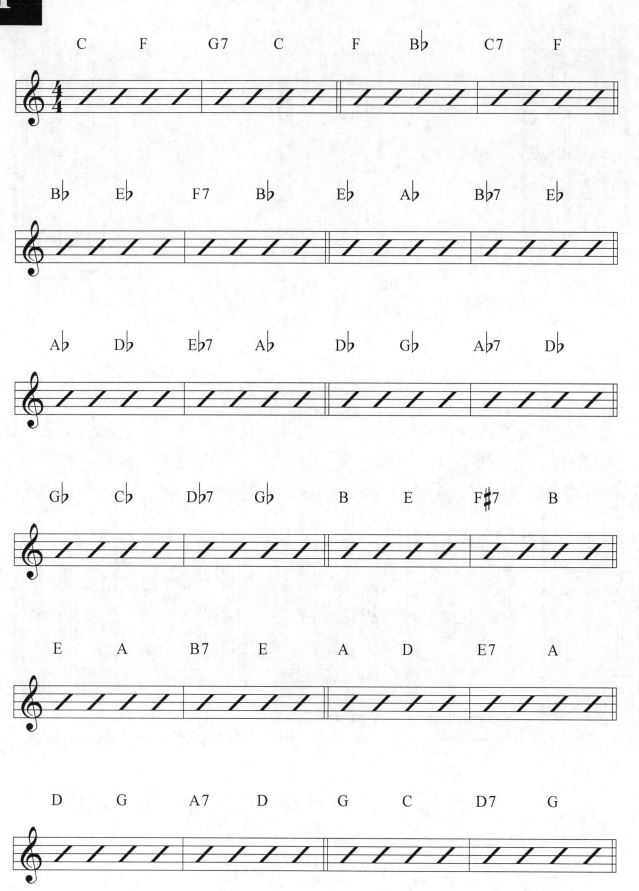

Minor Chords Review

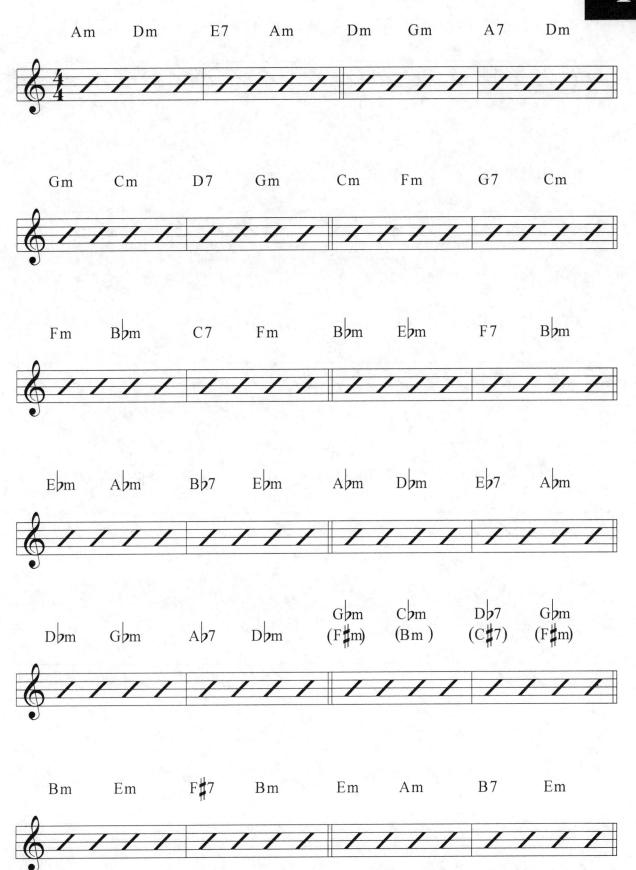

Major/Minor Review

Play Very Slowly

C Am F Dm   G G7 C   F Dm B♭ Gm   C C7 F

B♭ Gm E♭ Cm   F F7 B♭   E♭ Cm A♭ Fm   B♭ B♭7 E♭

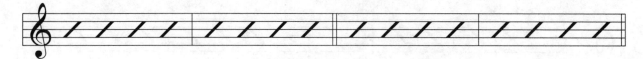

A♭ Fm D♭ B♭m   E♭ E♭7 A♭   D♭ B♭m G♭ E♭m   A♭ A♭7 D♭

G♭ E♭m B A♭m   D♭ D♭7 G♭   B G♯m E C♯m   F♯ F♯7 B

E C♯m A F♯m   B B7 E   A F♯m D Bm   E E7 A

D Bm G Em   A A7 D   G Em C Am   D D7 G

Zone II

In Zone II the 1st Finger of the Left Hand
will always be between the Third and Fifth Frets.

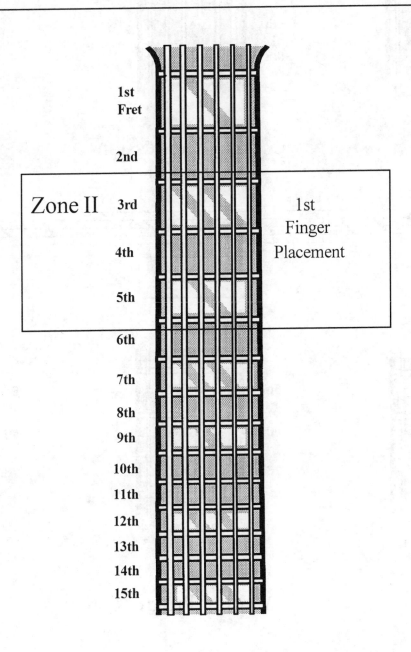

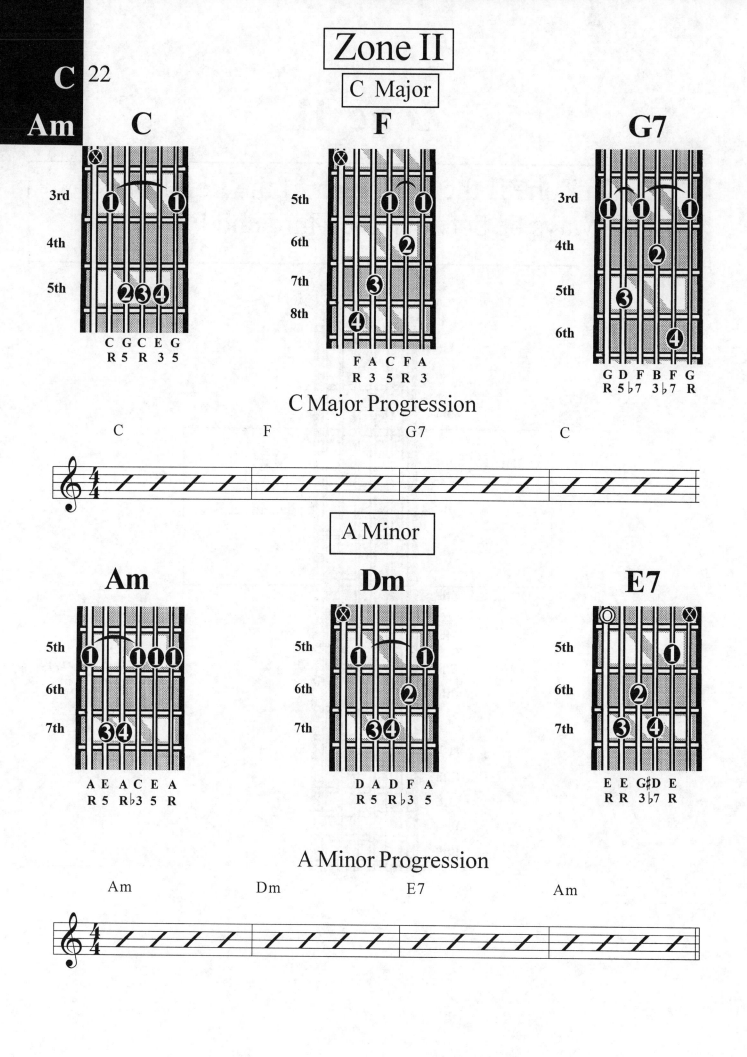

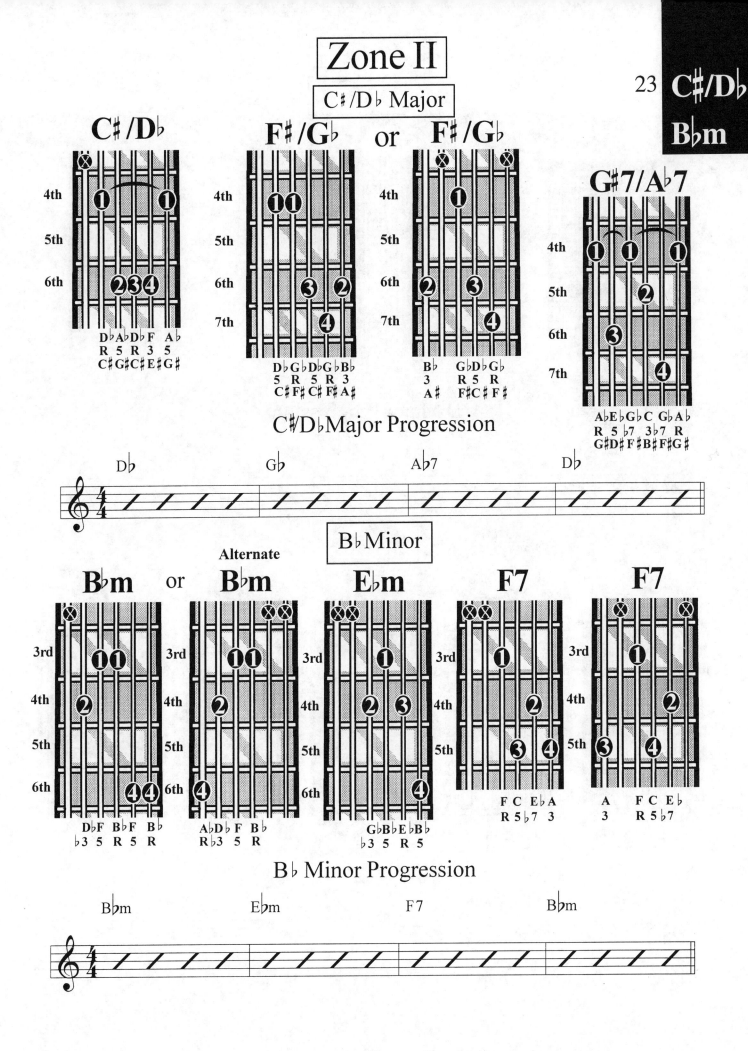

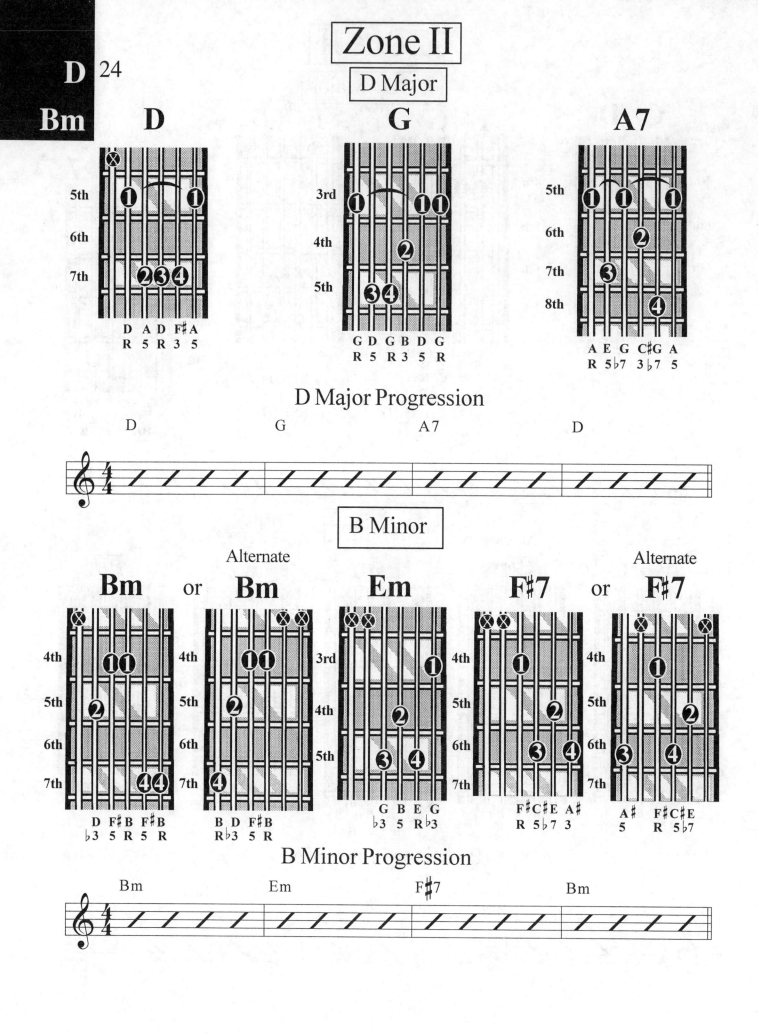

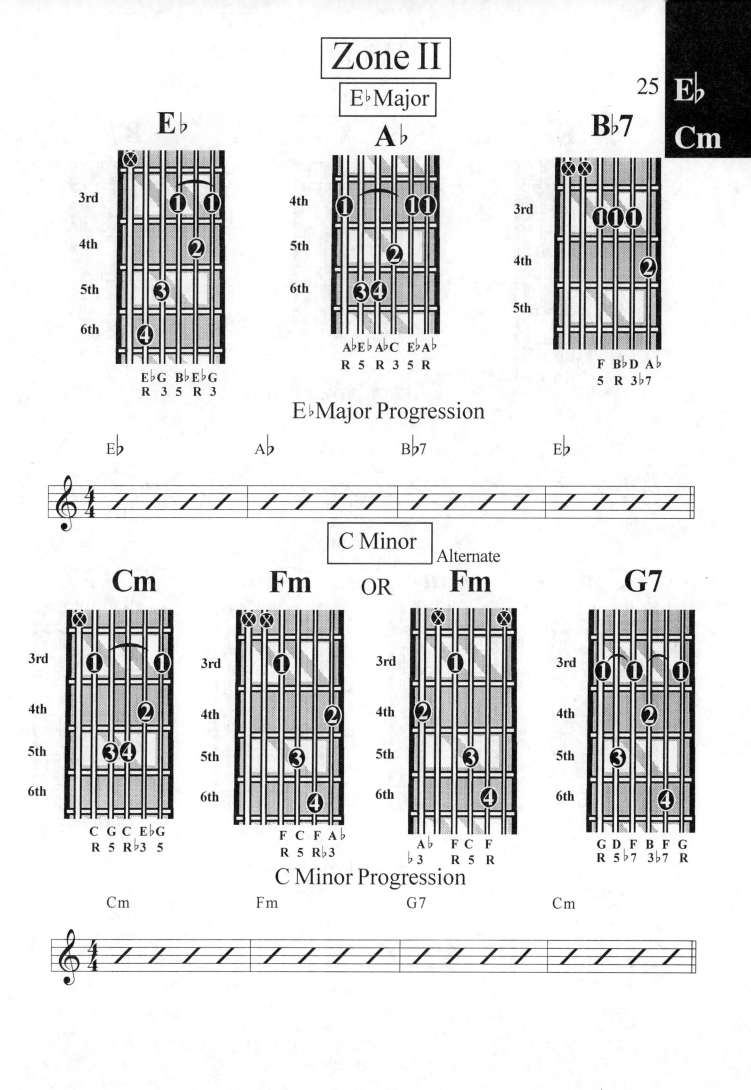

Zone II

E Major

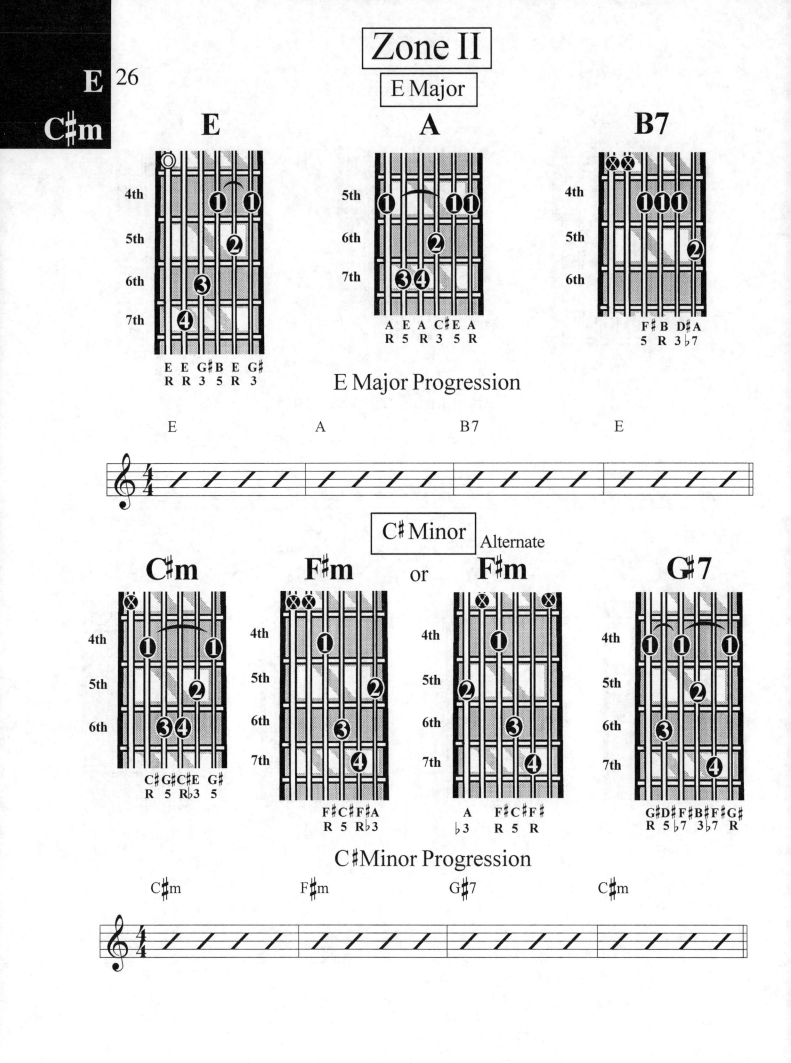

E

4th
5th
6th
7th

E E G#B E G#
R R 3 5 R 3

A

5th
6th
7th

A E A C#E A
R 5 R 3 5 R

B7

4th
5th
6th

F# B D#A
5 R 3 ♭7

E Major Progression

E   A   B7   E

C# Minor

C#m

4th
5th
6th

C#G#C#E G#
R 5 R♭3 5

F#m

4th
5th
6th
7th

F#C#F#A
R 5 R♭3

or

Alternate

F#m

4th
5th
6th
7th

A   F#C#F#
♭3 R 5 R

G#7

4th
5th
6th
7th

G#D#F#B#F#G#
R 5 ♭7 3♭7 R

C#Minor Progression

C#m   F#m   G#7   C#m

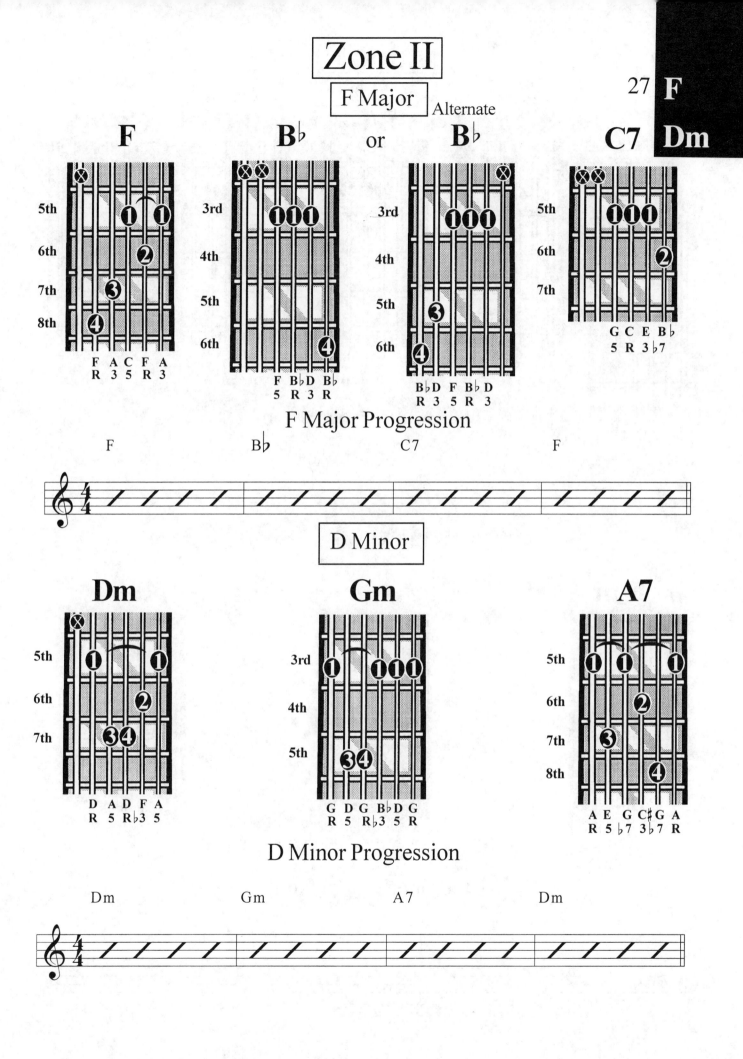

Zone II
F#/Gb Major

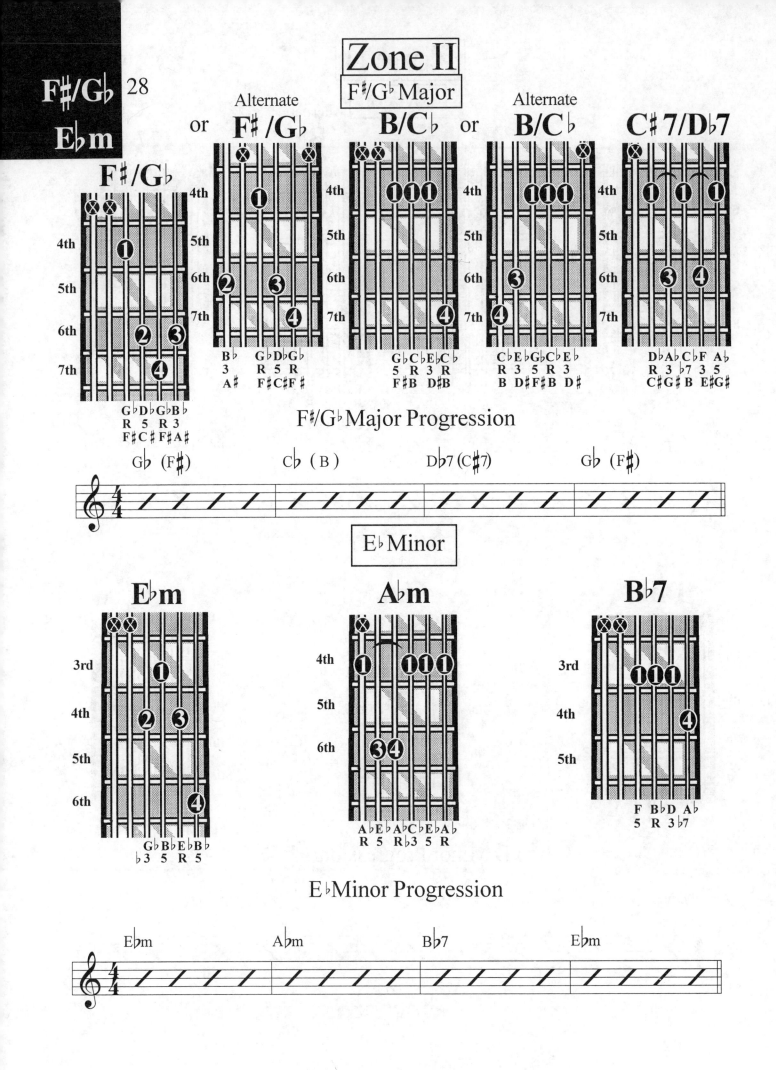

or **F#/Gb**   Alternate **F#/Gb**

B/Cb or   Alternate **B/Cb**

C# 7/Db7

F#/Gb

Gb Db Gb Bb
R 5 R 3
F# C# F# A#

Bb   Gb Db Gb
3   R 5 R
A#   F# C# F#

Gb Cb Eb Cb
5 R 3 R
F# B D# B

Cb Eb Gb Cb Eb
R 3 5 R 3
B D# F# B D#

Db Ab Cb F Ab
R 3 b7 3 5
C# G# B E# G#

F#/Gb Major Progression

Gb (F#)   Cb (B)   Db7 (C#7)   Gb (F#)

Eb Minor

Ebm

Gb Bb Eb Bb
b3 5 R 5

Abm

Ab Eb Ab Cb Eb Ab
R 5 R b3 5 R

Bb7

F Bb D Ab
5 R 3 b7

Eb Minor Progression

Ebm   Abm   Bb7   Ebm

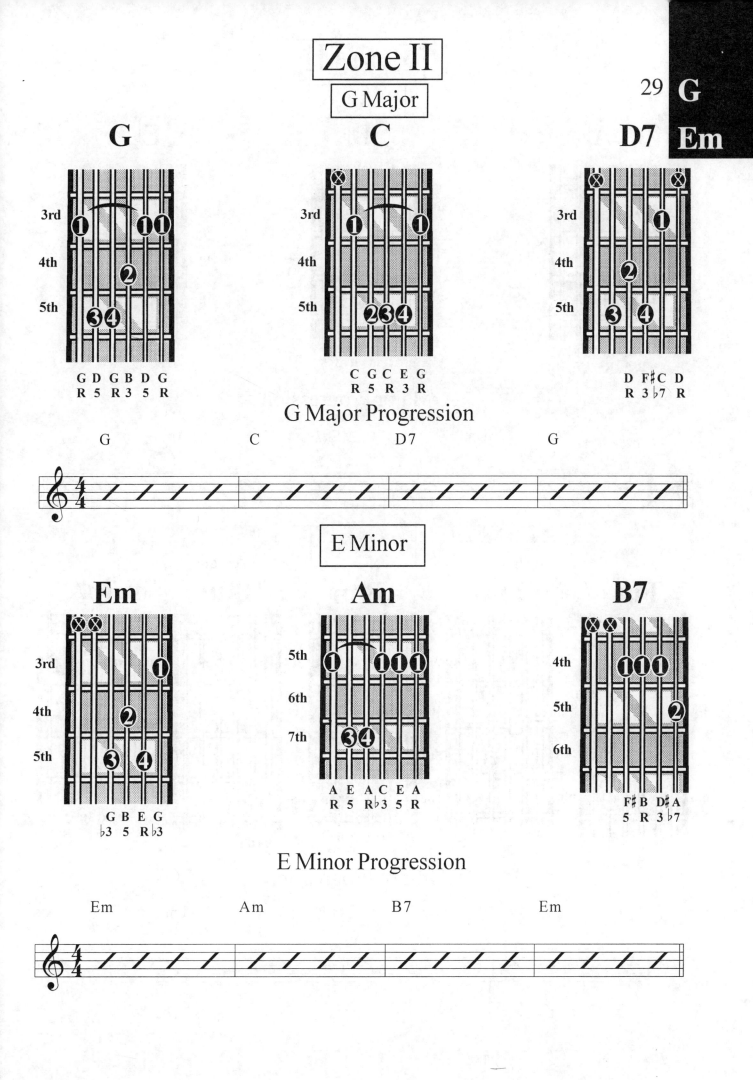

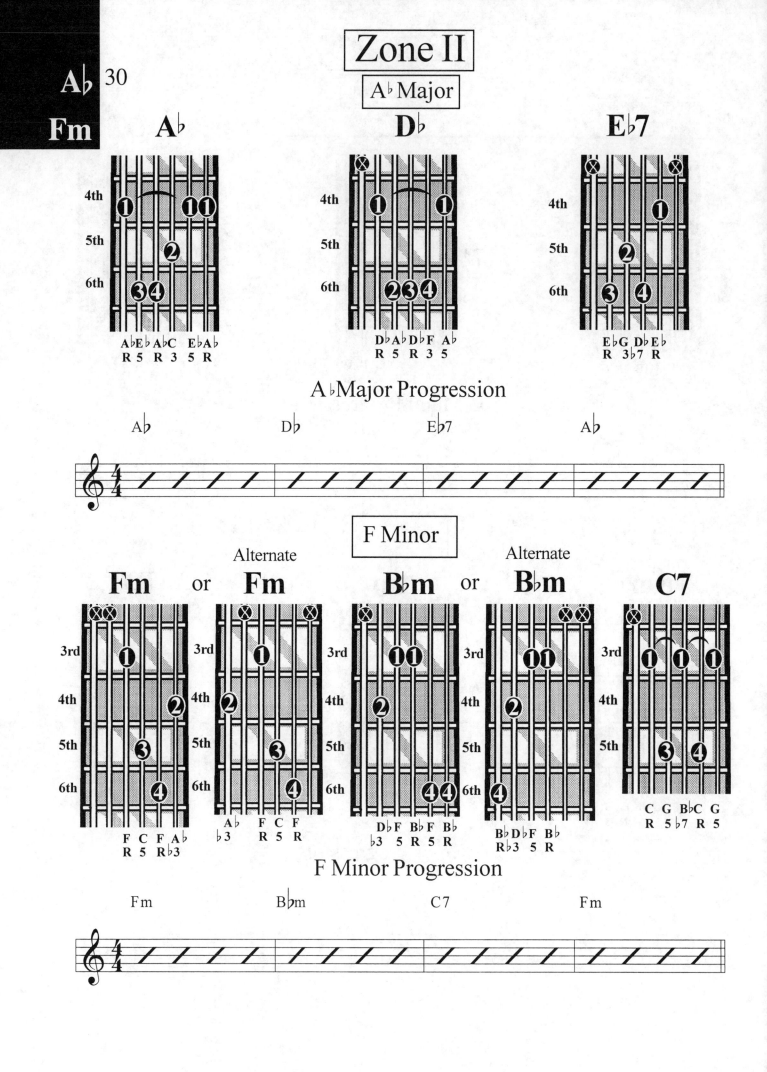

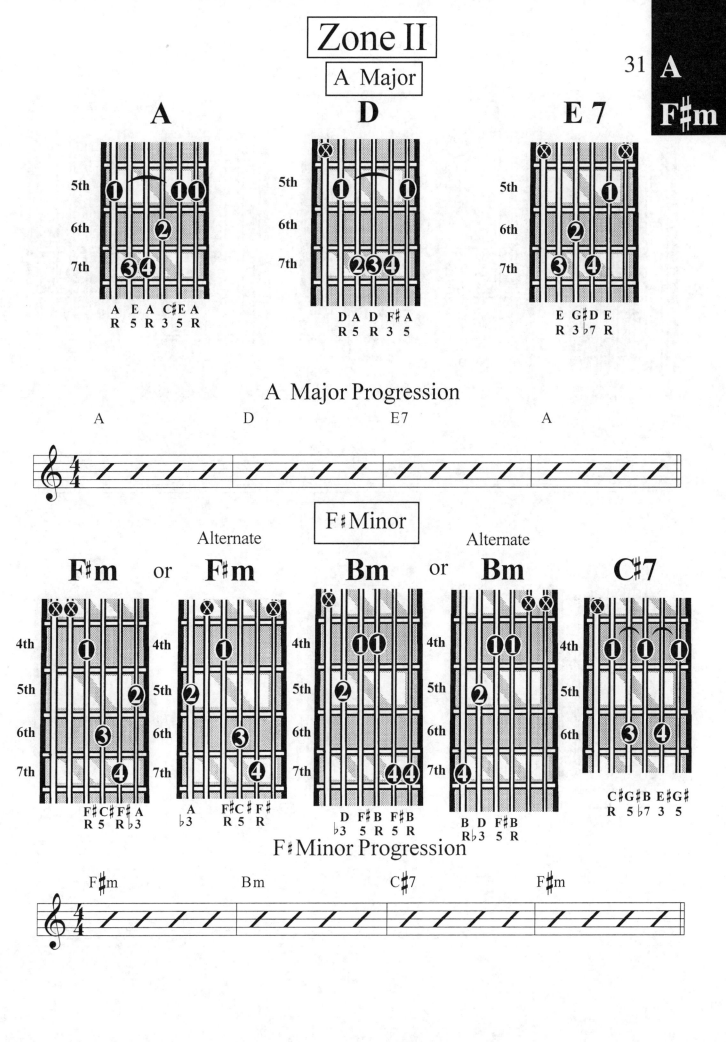

Zone II

B♭ Major

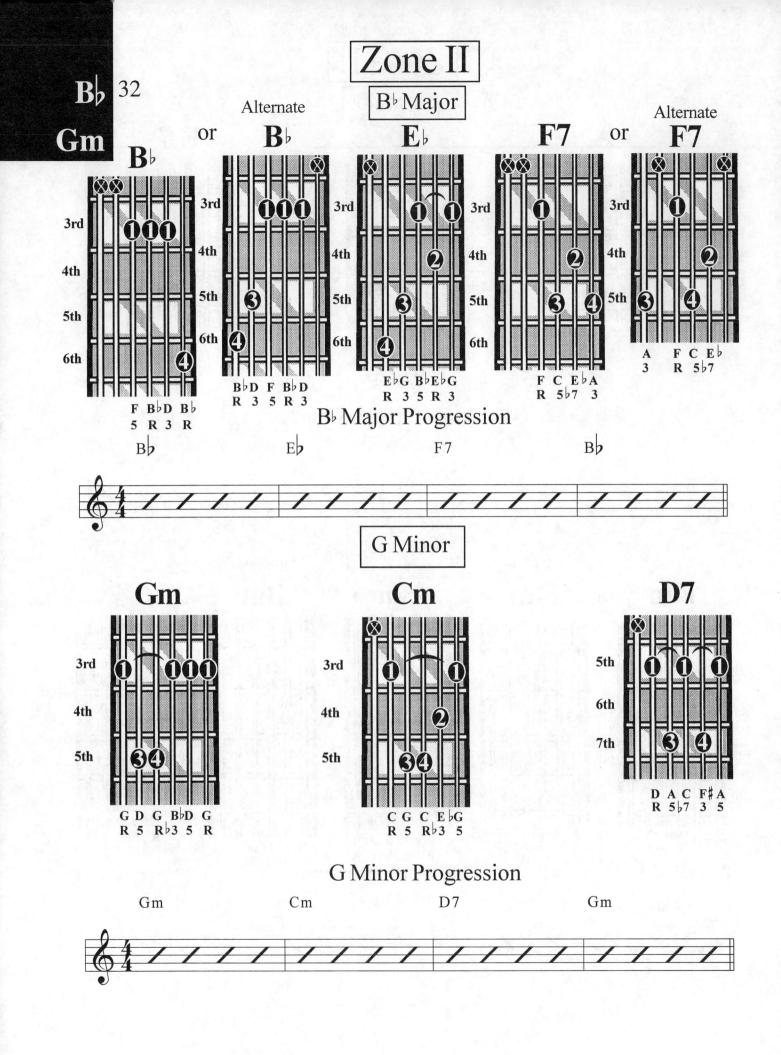

Alternate
or

B♭

B♭

E♭

F7

Alternate
or

F7

B♭ Major Progression

| B♭ | E♭ | F7 | B♭ |

G Minor

Gm

Cm

D7

G Minor Progression

| Gm | Cm | D7 | Gm |

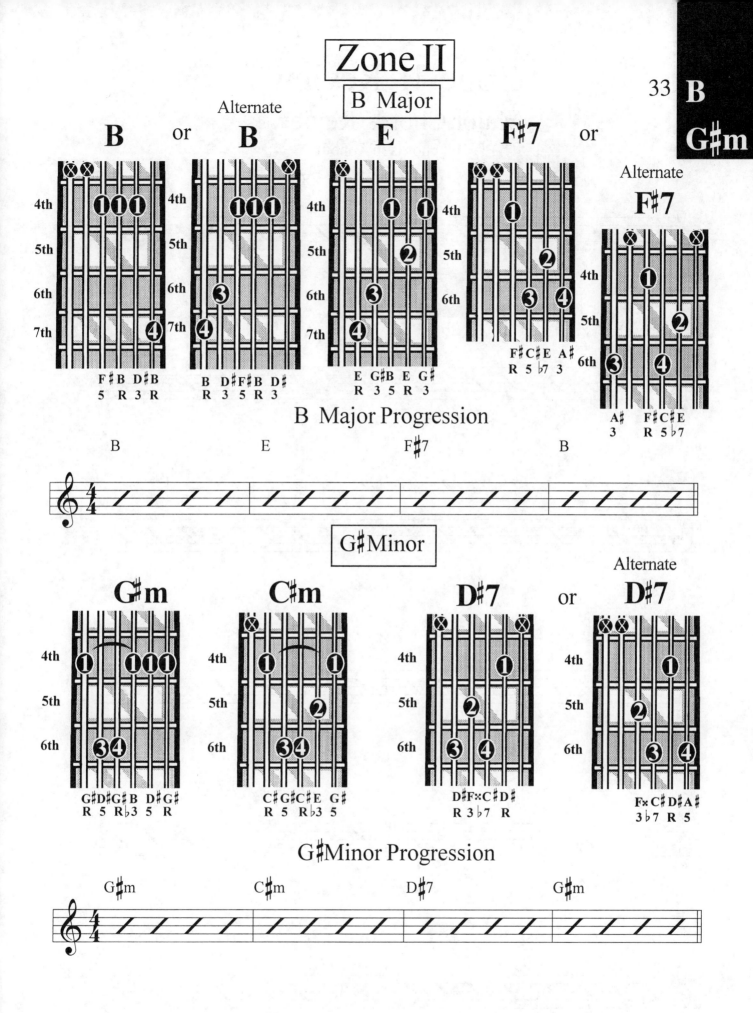

Zone II Review
Major Chords Review
* Play all chords in Zone II *

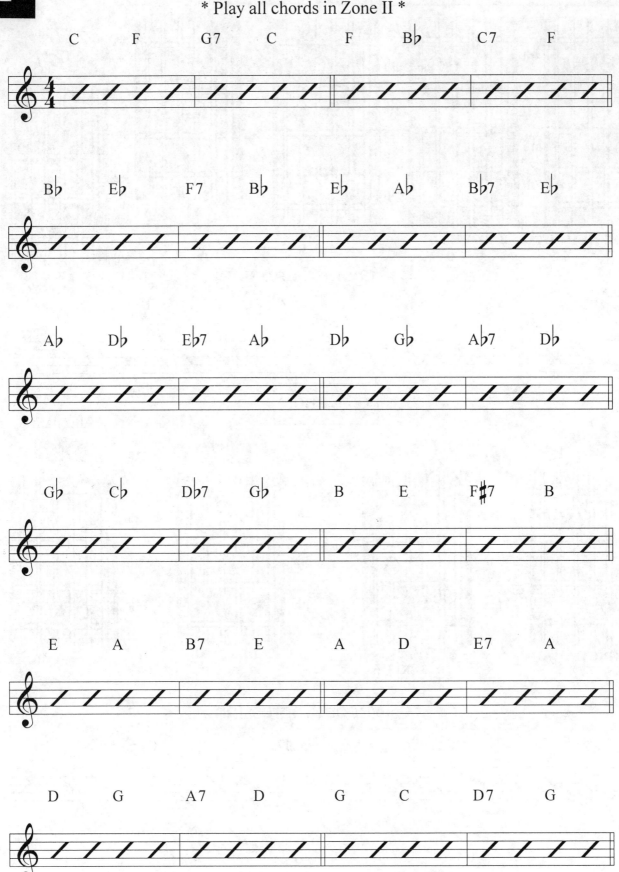

Minor Chords Review

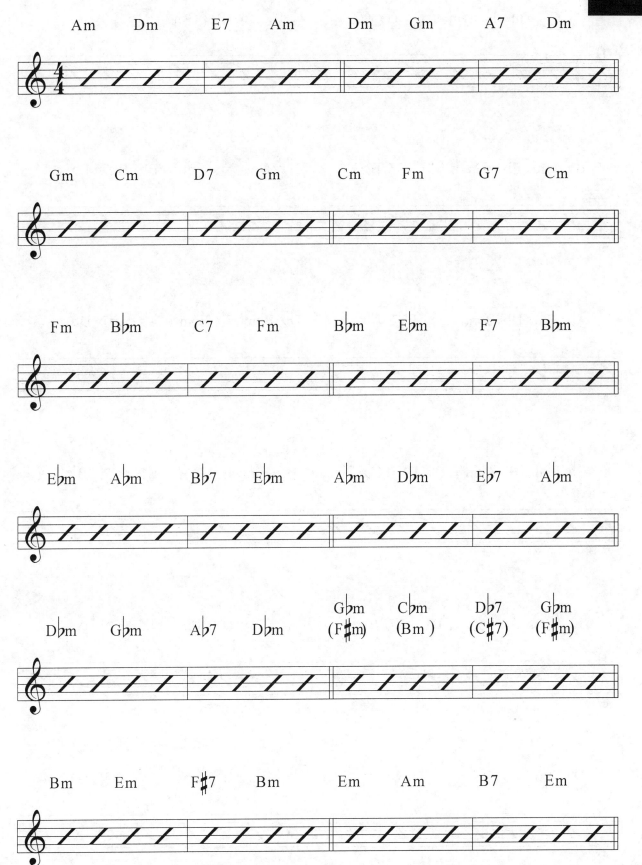

Major/Minor Review

Play Very Slowly

C Am F Dm G G7 C F Dm B♭ Gm C C7 F

B♭ Gm E♭ Cm F F7 B♭ E♭ Cm A♭ Fm B♭ B♭7 E♭

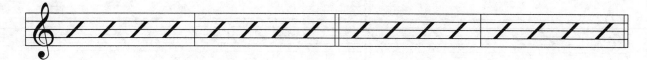

A♭ Fm D♭ B♭m E♭ E♭7 A♭ D♭ B♭m G♭ E♭m A♭ A♭7 D♭

G♭ E♭m B A♭m D♭ D♭7 G♭ B G♯m E C♯m F♯ F♯7 B

E C♯m A F♯m B B7 E A F♯m D Bm E E7 A

D Bm G Em A A7 D G Em C Am D D7 G

Zone III

In Zone III the 1st Finger of the Left Hand
will always be between the Fifth and Seventh Frets.

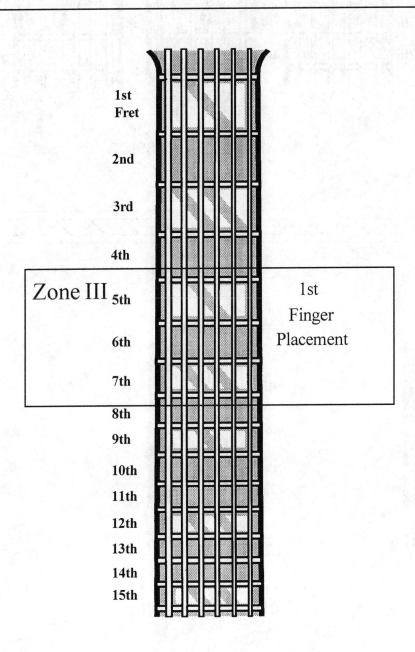

Zone III

1st
Fret

2nd

3rd

4th

5th

6th

7th

8th

9th

10th

11th

12th

13th

14th

15th

1st
Finger
Placement

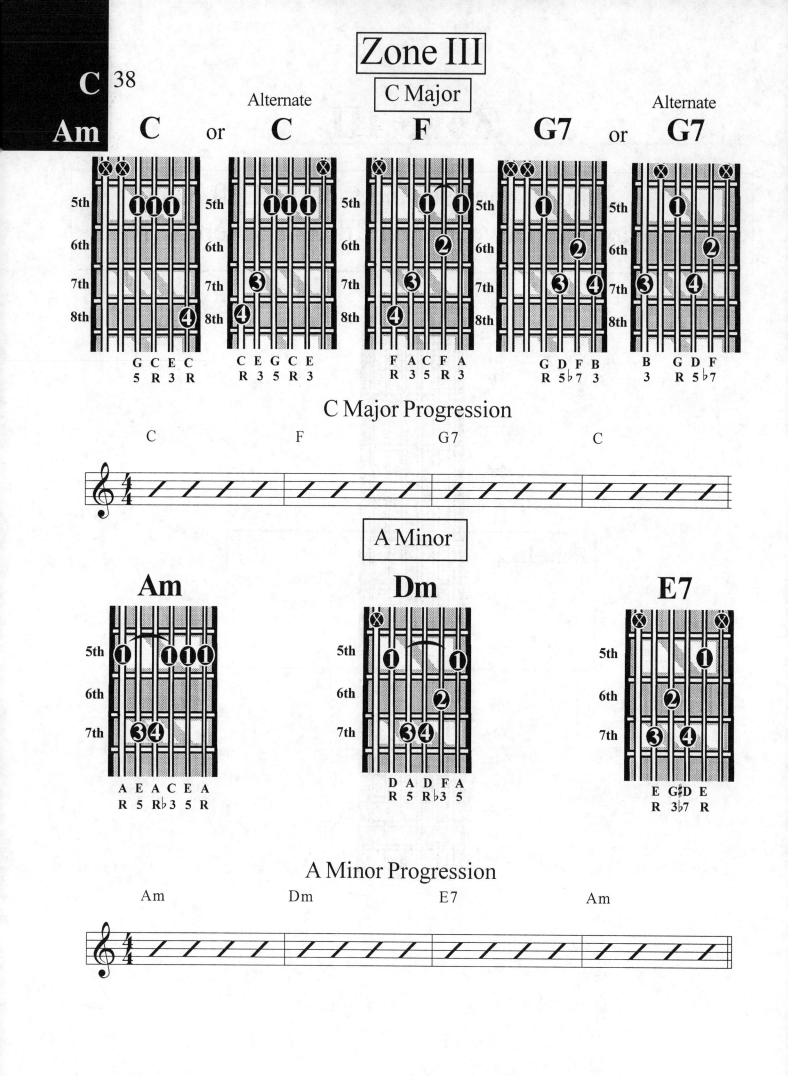

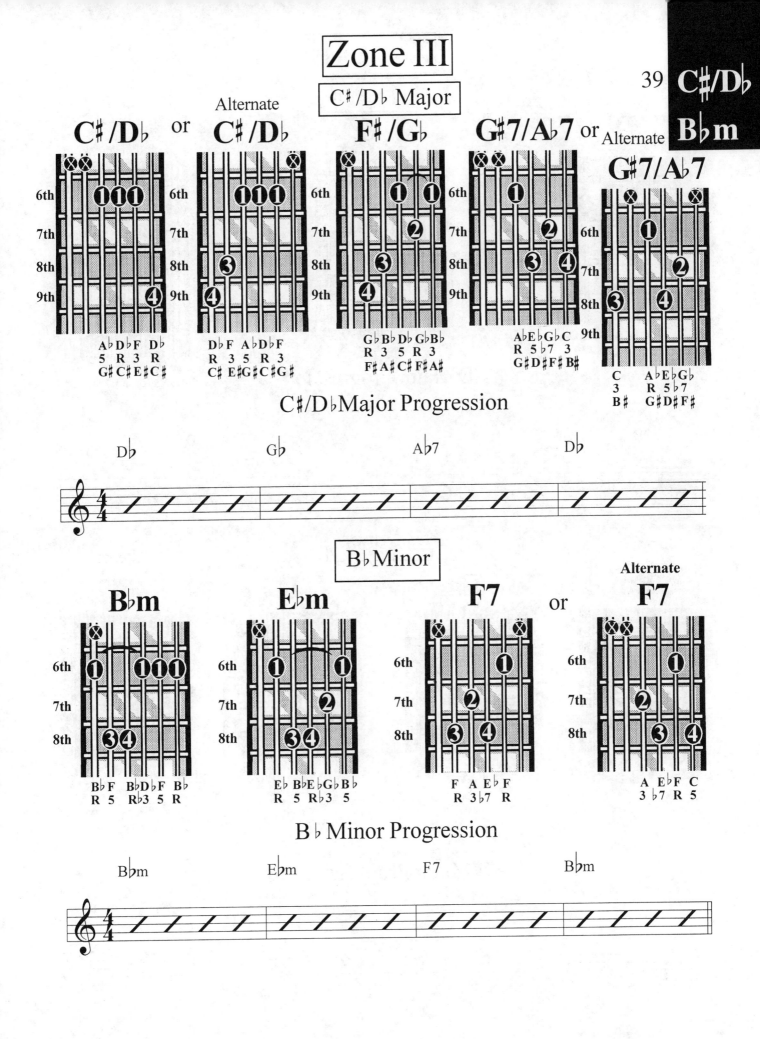

Zone III

C#/Db Major

C#/Db or C#/Db (Alternate) F#/Gb G#7/Ab7 or Bbm (Alternate)

G#7/Ab7

C#/Db Major Progression

Db   Gb   Ab7   Db

Bb Minor

Bbm   Ebm   F7 or F7 (Alternate)

Bb Minor Progression

Bbm   Ebm   F7   Bbm

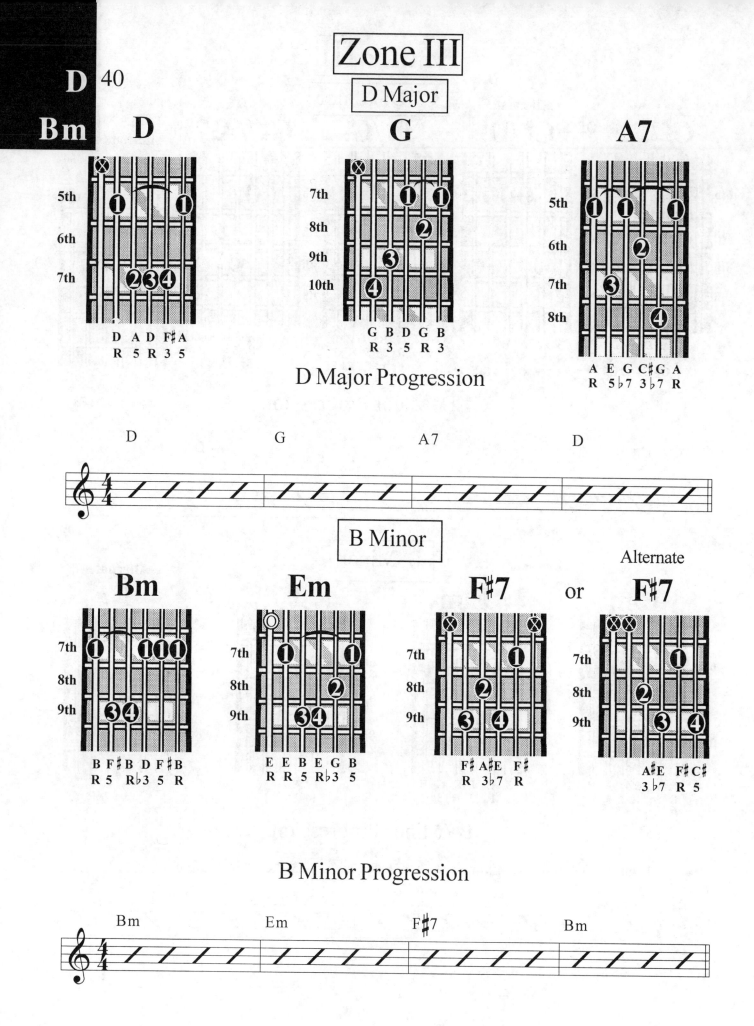

Zone III
D Major

D Major Progression

B Minor

B Minor Progression

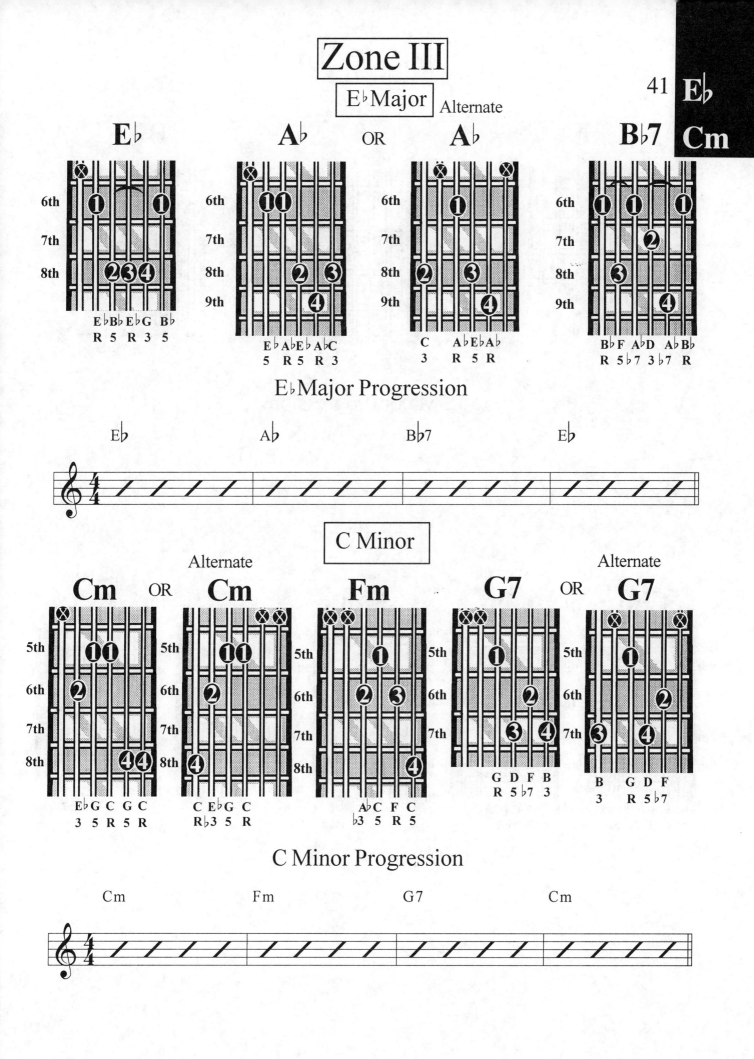

Zone III

Eb Major

41 Eb / Cm

Eb   **Ab**   OR   **Ab**   **Bb7**

Eb Major Progression

Eb   Ab   Bb7   Eb

C Minor

Cm   OR   **Cm**   **Fm**   **G7**   OR   **G7**

C Minor Progression

Cm   Fm   G7   Cm

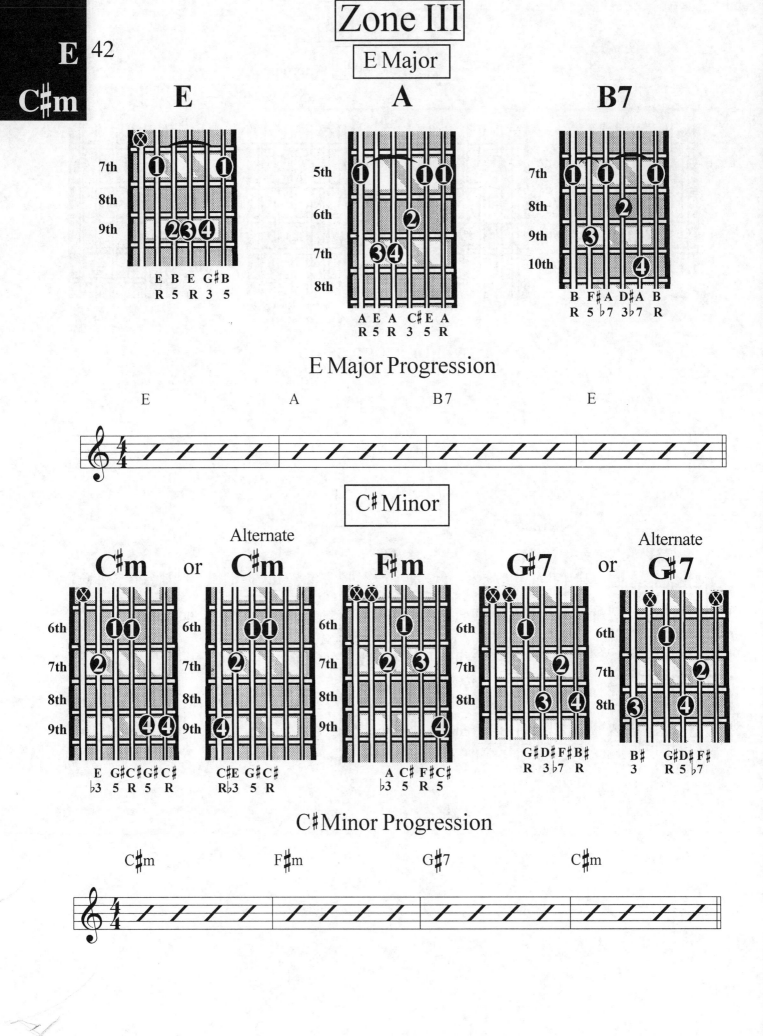

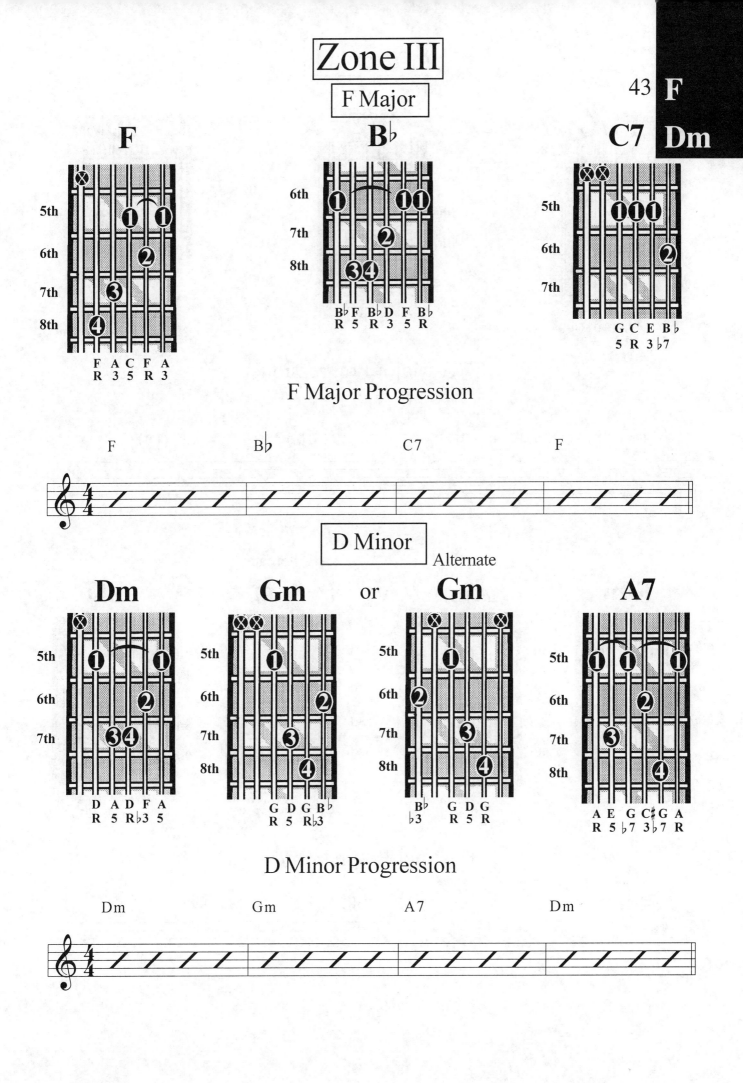

Zone III
F#/G♭ Major

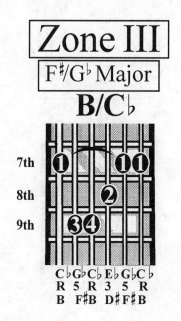

F#/G♭

6th
7th
8th
9th

G♭ B♭ D♭ G♭ B♭
R 3 5 R 3
F# A# C# F# A#

B/C♭

7th
8th
9th

C♭ G♭ C♭ E♭ G♭ C♭
R 5 R 3 5 R
B F# B D# F# B

C#7/D♭7

6th
7th

A♭ D♭ F C♭
5 R 3 ♭7
G# C# E# B

F#/G♭ Major Progression

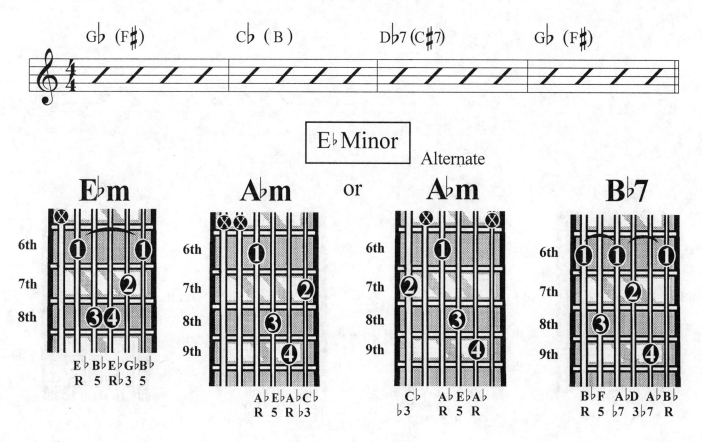

G♭ (F#)   C♭ (B)   D♭7 (C#7)   G♭ (F#)

E♭ Minor

Alternate or

E♭m

6th
7th
8th

E♭ B♭ E♭ G♭ B♭
R 5 R ♭3 5

A♭m

6th
7th
8th
9th

A♭ E♭ A♭ C♭
R 5 R ♭3

A♭m

6th
7th
8th
9th

C♭ A♭ E♭ A♭
♭3 R 5 R

B♭7

6th
7th
8th
9th

B♭ F A♭ D A♭ B♭
R 5 ♭7 3 ♭7 R

E♭ Minor Progression

E♭m   A♭m   B♭7   E♭m

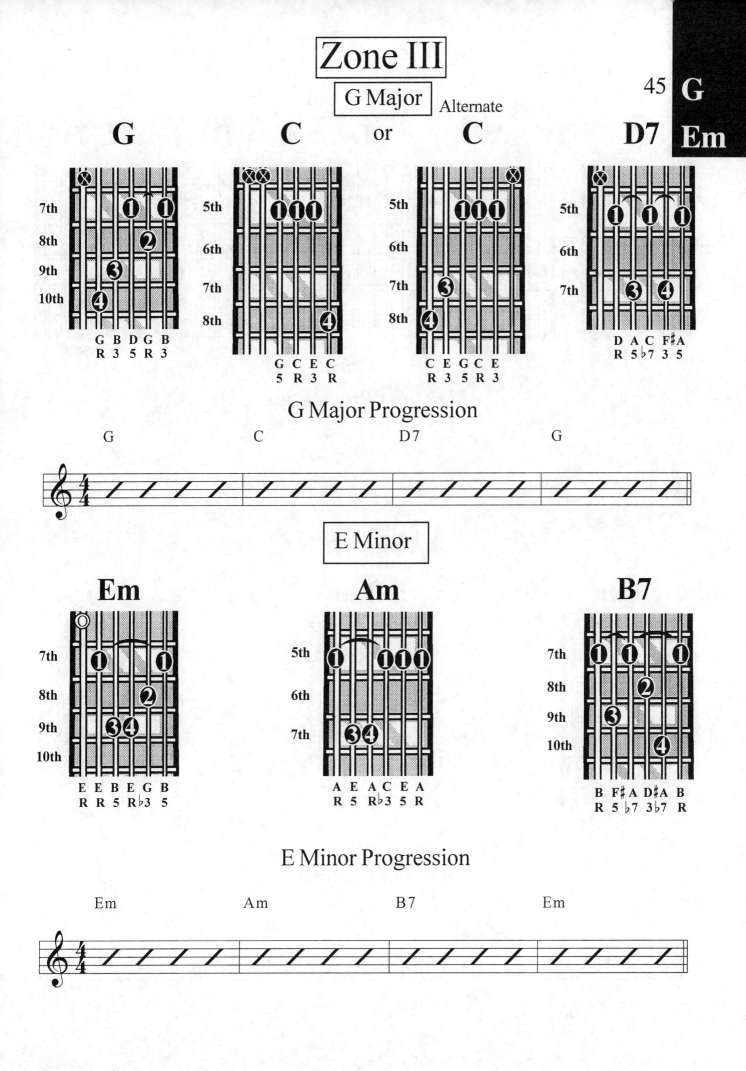

Zone III

G Major | Alternate

G Major Progression

E Minor

E Minor Progression

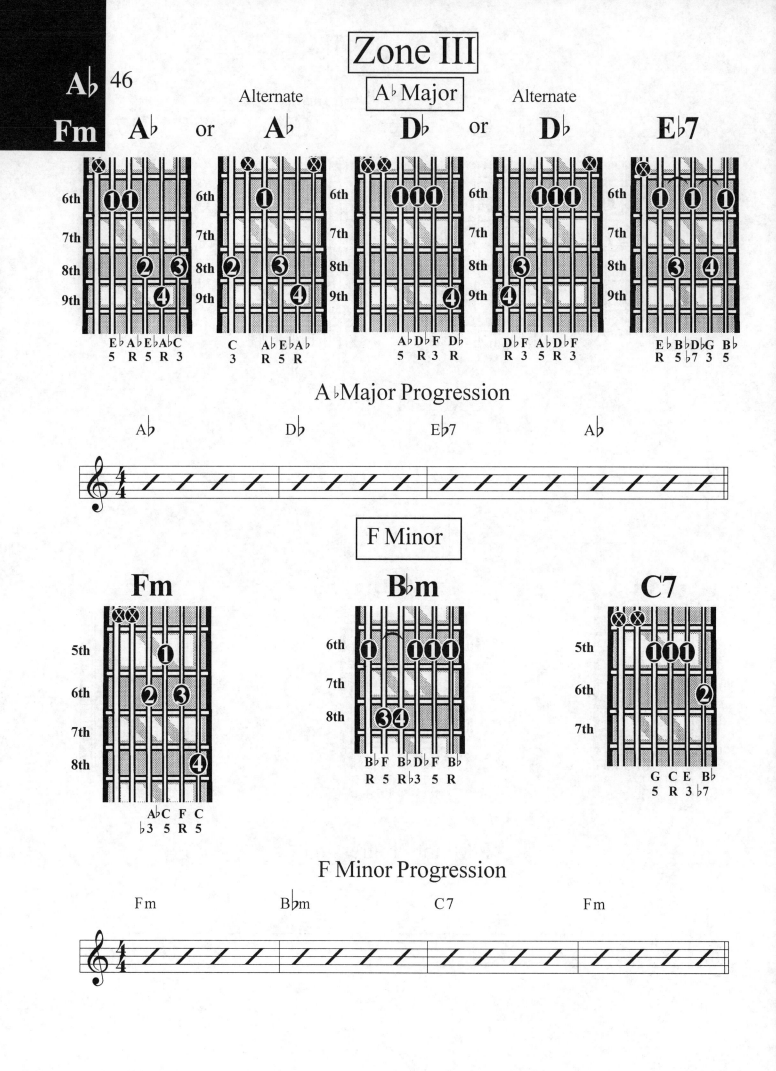

Zone III

A Major

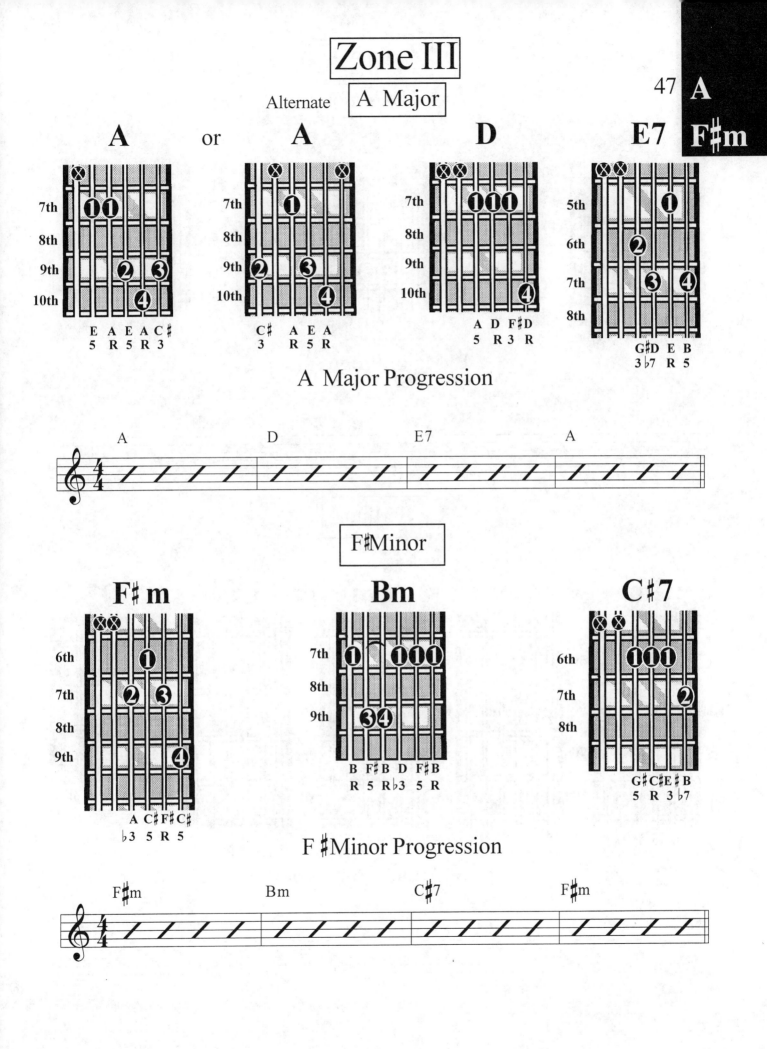

Alternate

A or **A**   **D**   **E7**   **A** **F♯m**

A Major Progression

A   D   E7   A

F♯Minor

F♯m   **Bm**   **C♯7**

F♯Minor Progression

F♯m   Bm   C♯7   F♯m

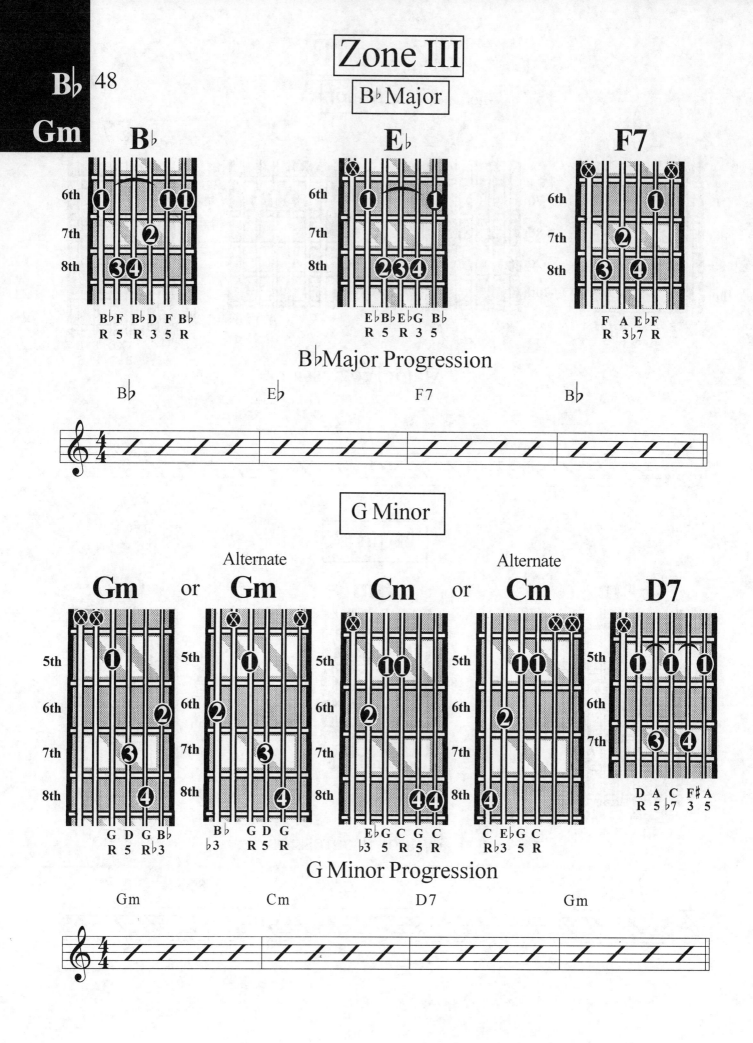

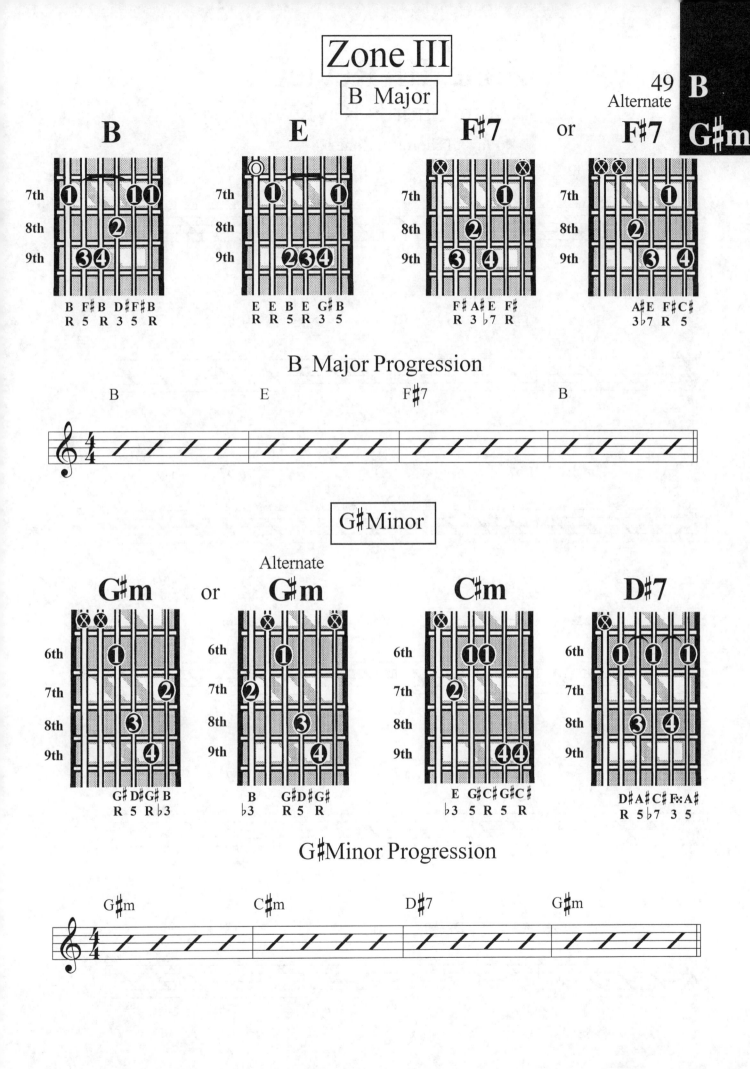

Zone III Review
Major Chords Review
* Play all chords in Zone III *

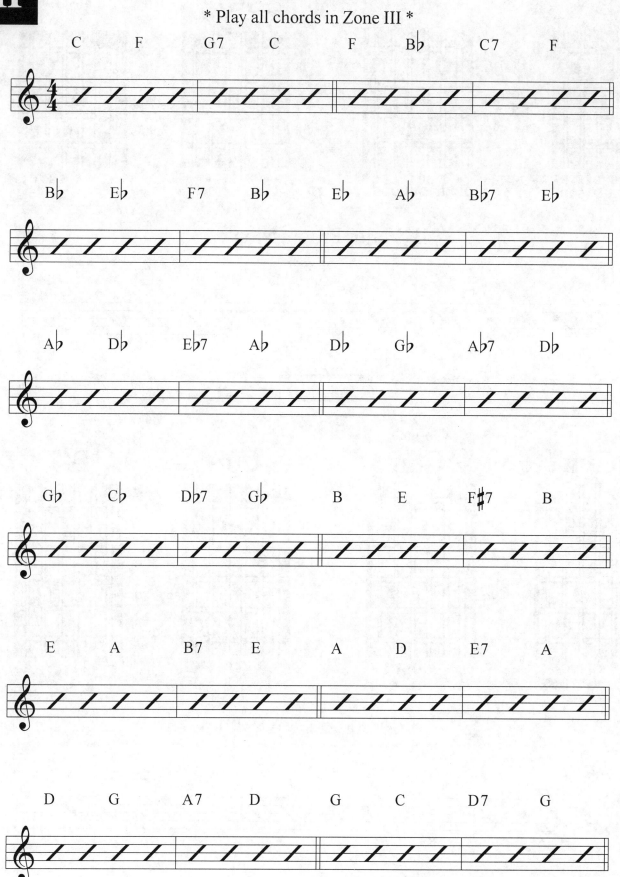

Minor Chords Review

III

Major/Minor Review

Play Very Slowly

C Am F Dm   G G7 C   F Dm B♭ Gm   C C7 F

B♭ Gm E♭ Cm   F F7 B♭   E♭ Cm A♭ Fm   B♭ B♭7 E♭

A♭ Fm D♭ B♭m   E♭ E♭7 A♭   D♭ B♭m G♭ E♭m   A♭ A♭7 D♭

G♭ E♭m B A♭m   D♭ D♭7 G♭   B G♯m E C♯m   F♯ F♯7 B

E C♯m A F♯m   B B7 E   A F♯m D Bm   E E7 A

D Bm G Em   A A7 D   G Em C Am   D D7 G

Zone IV

In Zone IV the 1st Finger of the Left Hand
will always be between the Seventh and Ninth Frets.

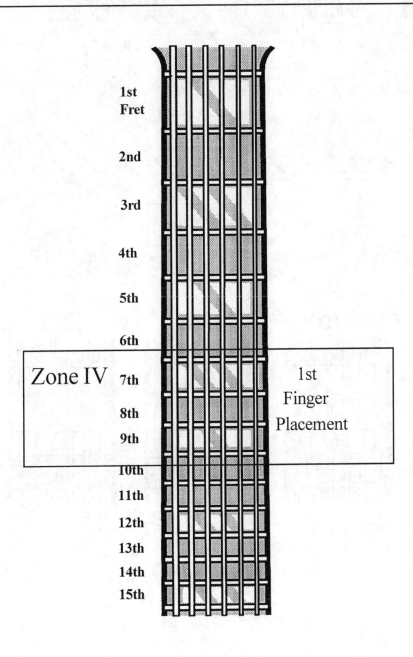

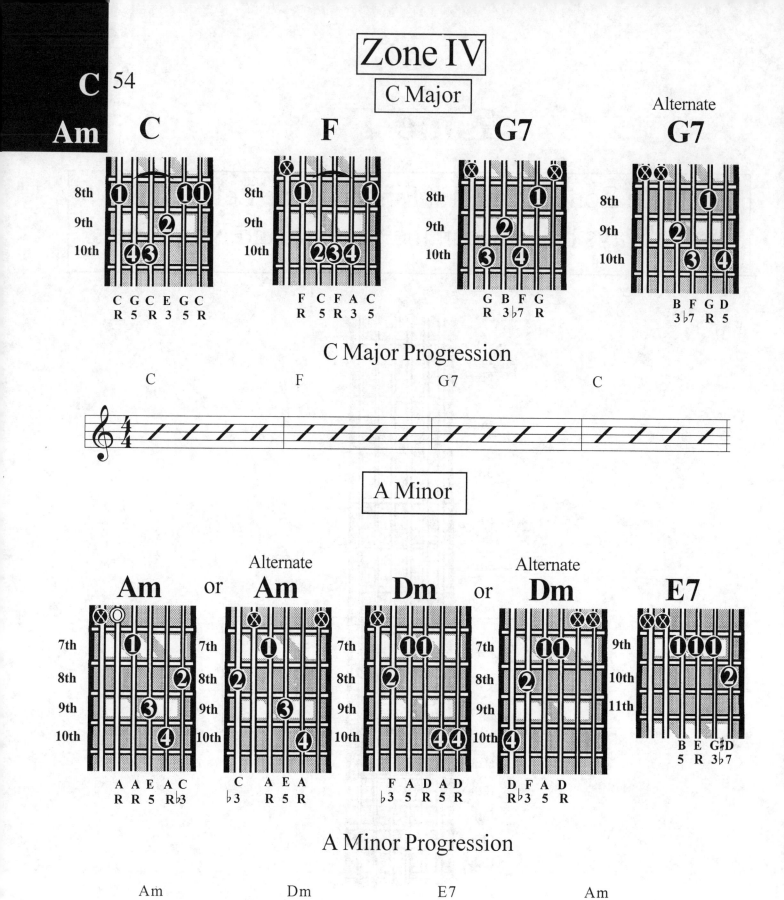

Zone IV

C Major

C Major Progression

A Minor

A Minor Progression

C# /D♭ Major

Alternate

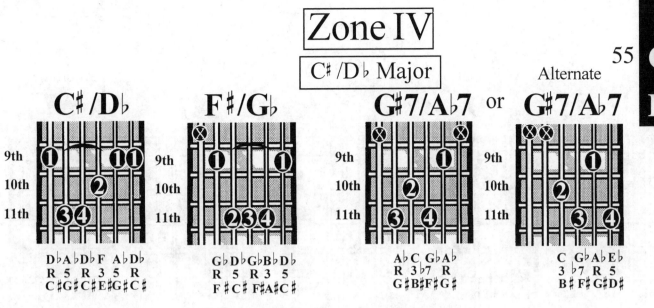

C# /D♭

F#/G♭

G#7/A♭7 or **G#7/A♭7**

9th ① ① ①
10th ②
11th ③ ④

D♭A♭D♭F A♭D♭
R 5 R 3 5 R
C#G#C#E#G#C#

9th ① ①
10th
11th ② ③ ④

G♭D♭G♭B♭D♭
R 5 R 3 5
F# C# F#A#C#

9th ①
10th ②
11th ③ ④

A♭ C G♭A♭
R 3 ♭7 R
G#B#F#G#

9th ①
10th ②
11th ③ ④

C G♭A E♭
3 ♭7 R 5
B# F#G#D#

C# /D♭ Major Progression

D♭ (C#)   G♭ (F#)   A♭7 (G#7)   D♭ (C#)

B♭ Minor

B♭m or **B♭m**   **E♭m** or **E♭m**   **F7**

Alternate   Alternate

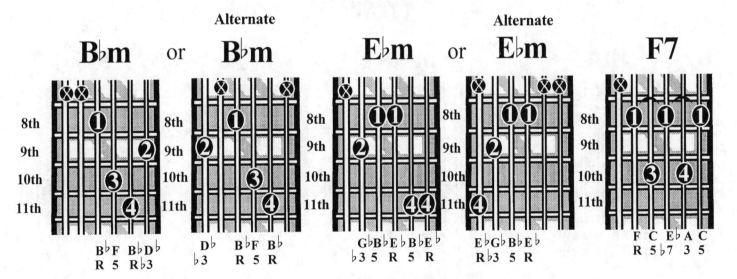

8th ①
9th ②
10th ③
11th ④

B♭F B♭D♭
R 5 R♭3

8th ①
9th ②
10th ③
11th ④

D♭ B♭F B♭
♭3 R 5 R

8th ① ①
9th ②
10th
11th ④ ④

G♭B♭E♭ B♭E♭
♭3 5 R 5 R

8th ① ①
9th ②
10th
11th ④

E♭G♭ B♭E♭
R♭3 5 R

8th ① ① ①
9th
10th ③ ④
11th

F C E♭A C
R 5 ♭7 3 5

B♭ Minor Progression

B♭m   E♭m   F7   B♭m

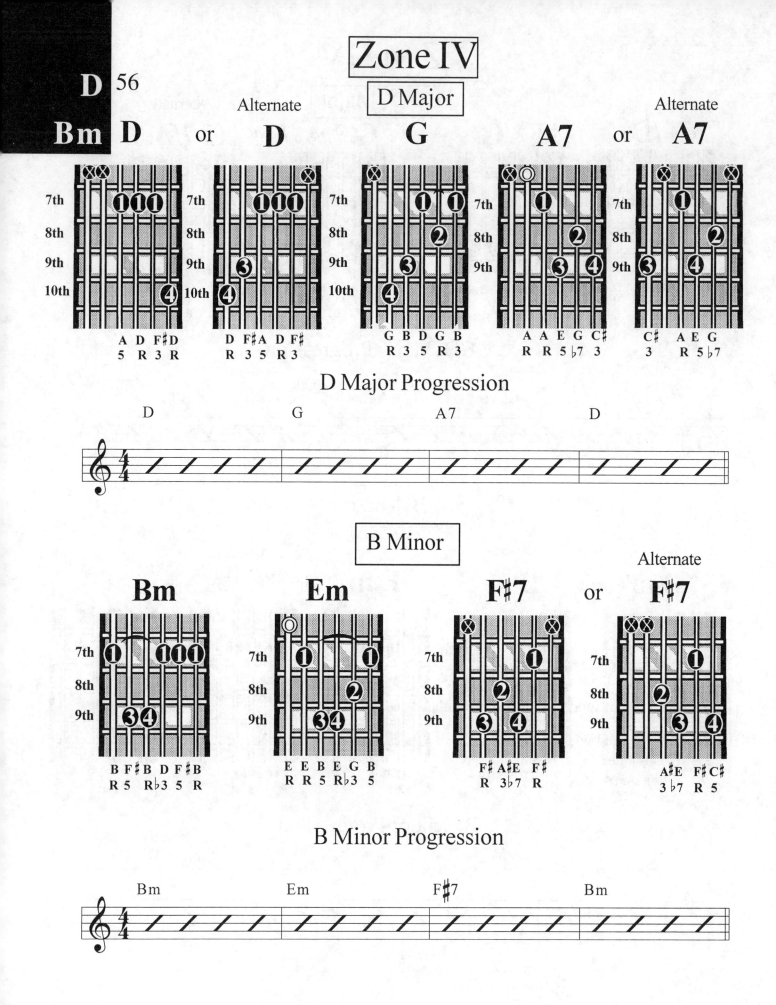

Zone IV

Eb Major

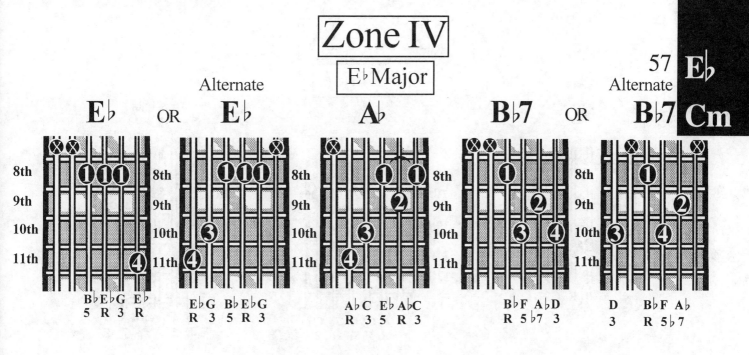

Eb Major Progression

| Eb | Ab | Bb7 | Eb |

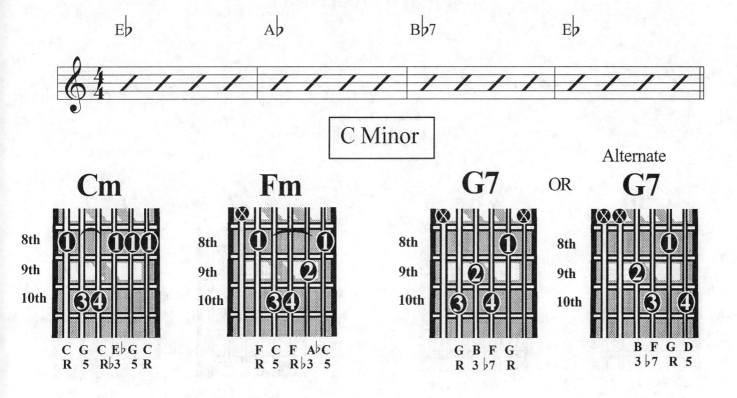

C Minor

C Minor Progression

| Cm | Fm | G7 | Cm |

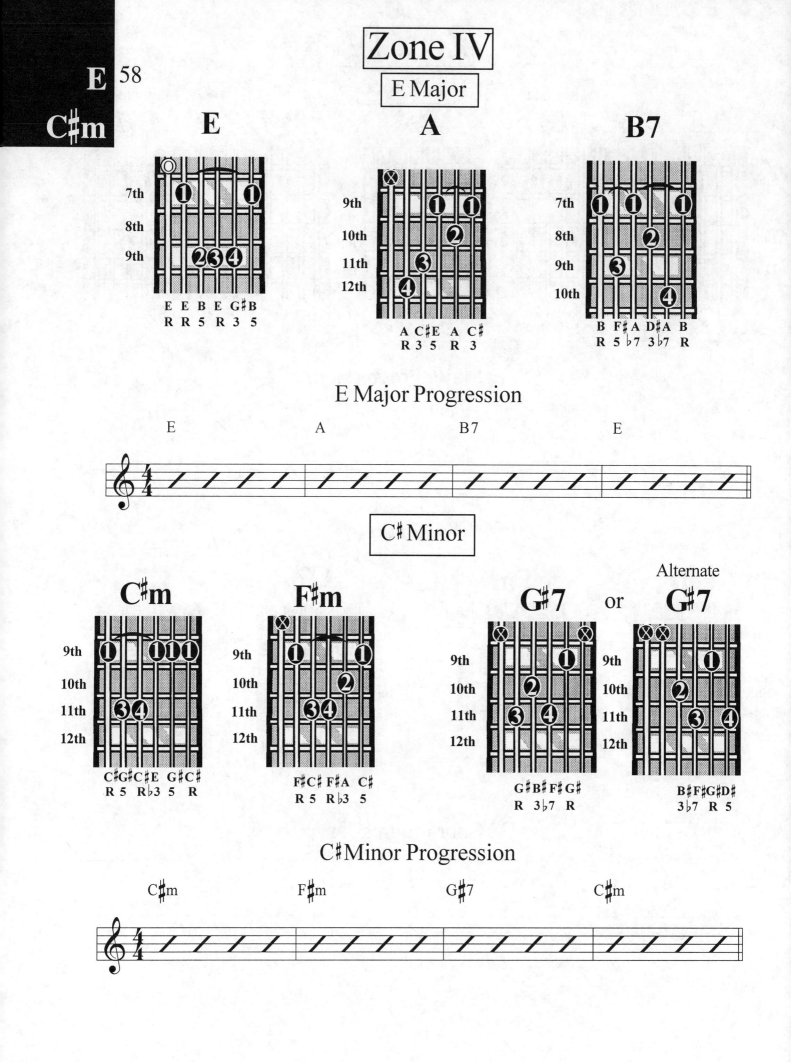

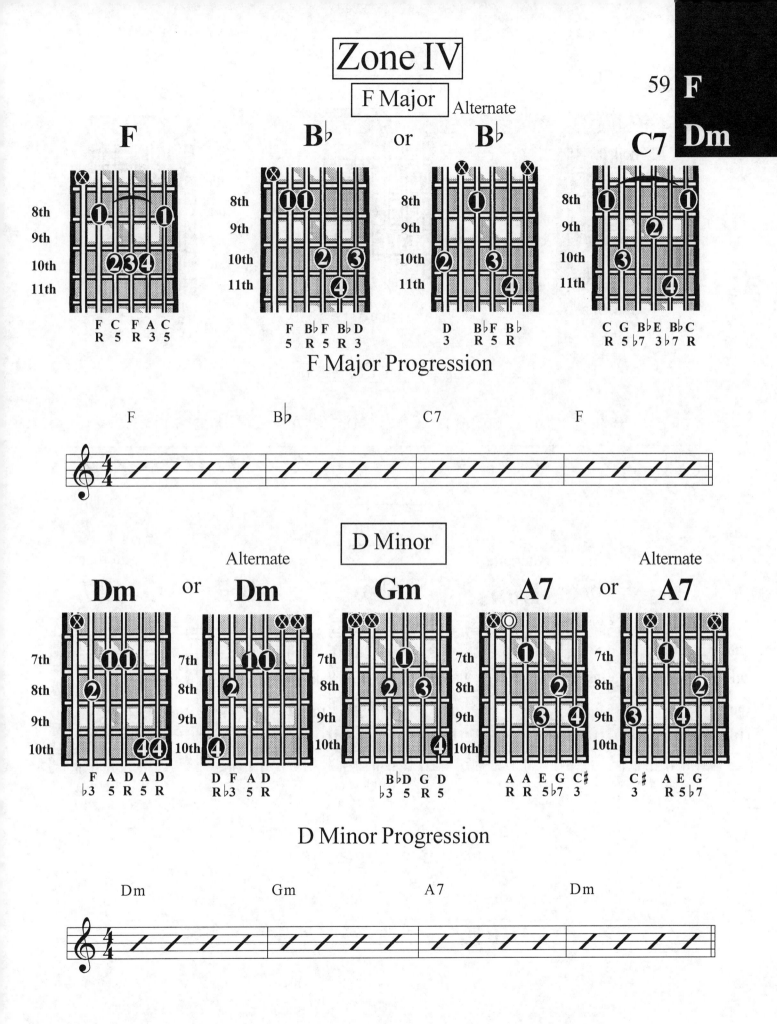

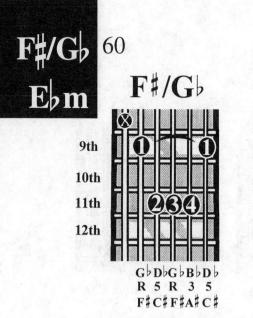

Zone IV
F#/Gb Major

F#/Gb

B/Cb

C#7/Db7

F#/Gb Major Progression

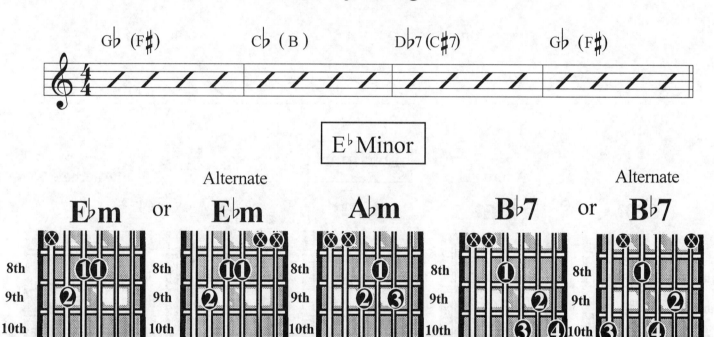

Gb (F#)   Cb (B)   Db7 (C#7)   Gb (F#)

Eb Minor

Ebm   or   Ebm (Alternate)   Abm   Bb7   or   Bb7 (Alternate)

Eb Minor Progression

Ebm   Abm   Bb7   Ebm

Zone IV

G Major

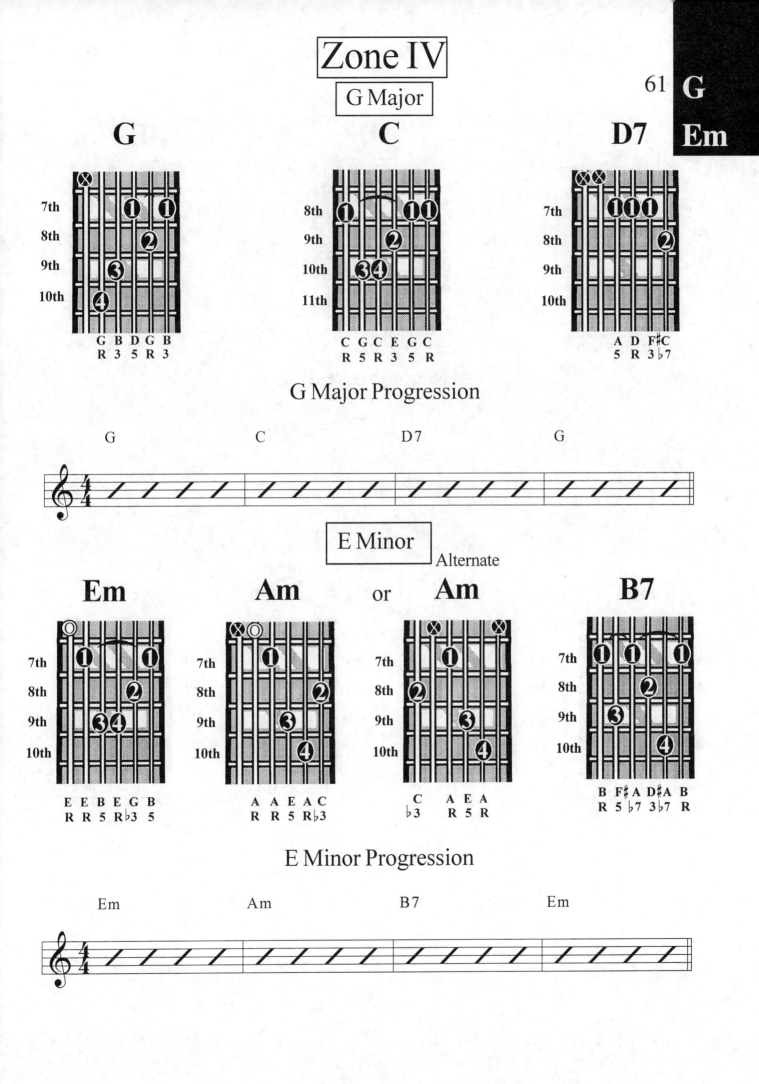

G

7th
8th
9th
10th

① ①
②
③
④

G B D G B
R 3 5 R 3

C

8th
9th
10th
11th

① ① ①
②
③ ④

C G C E G C
R 5 R 3 5 R

D7

7th
8th
9th
10th

① ① ① ①
②

A D F# C
5 R 3 ♭7

G Major Progression

G   C   D7   G

E Minor

Em

7th
8th
9th
10th

① ①
②
③ ④

E E B E G B
R R 5 R ♭3 5

Am

7th
8th
9th
10th

①
②
③
④

A A E A C
R R 5 R ♭3

or   Alternate

Am

7th
8th
9th
10th

①
②
③
④

C   A E A
♭3   R 5 R

B7

7th
8th
9th
10th

① ① ①   ①
②
③
④

B F# A D# A B
R 5 ♭7 3 ♭7 R

E Minor Progression

Em   Am   B7   Em

Fm

Zone IV
Ab Major

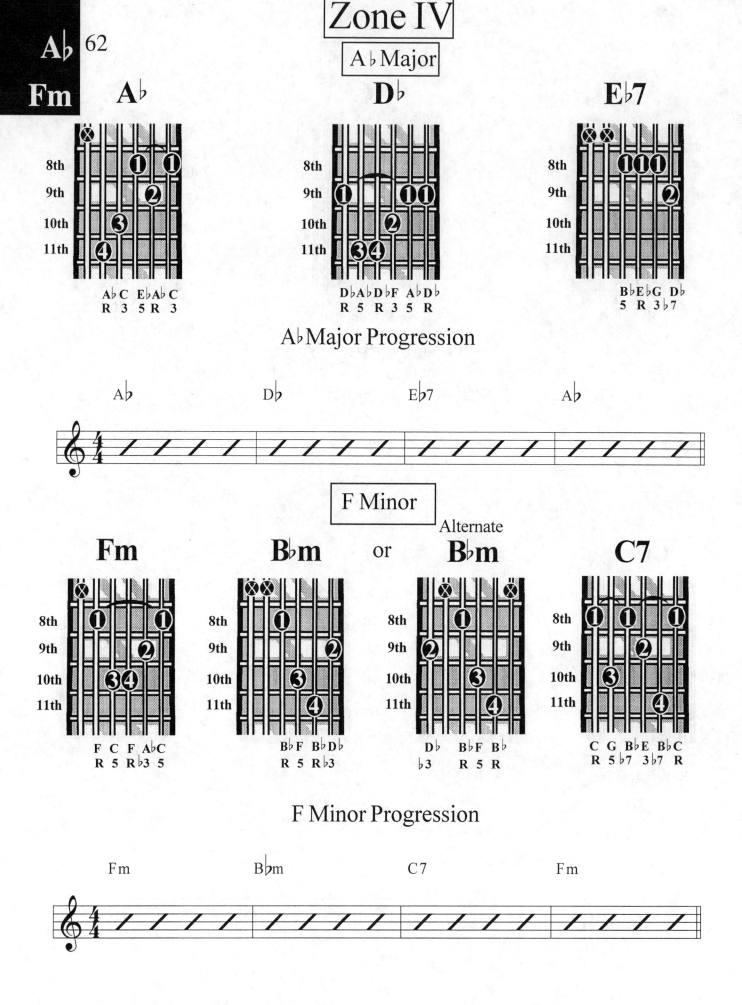

Ab   Db   Eb7

Ab Major Progression

Ab   Db   Eb7   Ab

F Minor

Fm   Bbm   or   Alternate Bbm   C7

F Minor Progression

Fm   Bbm   C7   Fm

Zone IV

A Major | Alternate

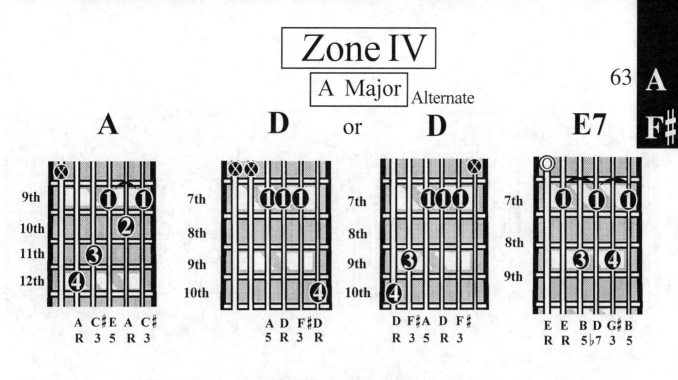

A   **D**   or   **D**   **E7**

A   F♯m

```
A    C♯ E  A  C♯        A  D  F♯ D        D  F♯ A  D  F♯        E  E  B  D  G♯ B
R    3  5  R  3         5  R  3  R         R  3  5  R  3         R  R  5 ♭7 3  5
```

A Major Progression

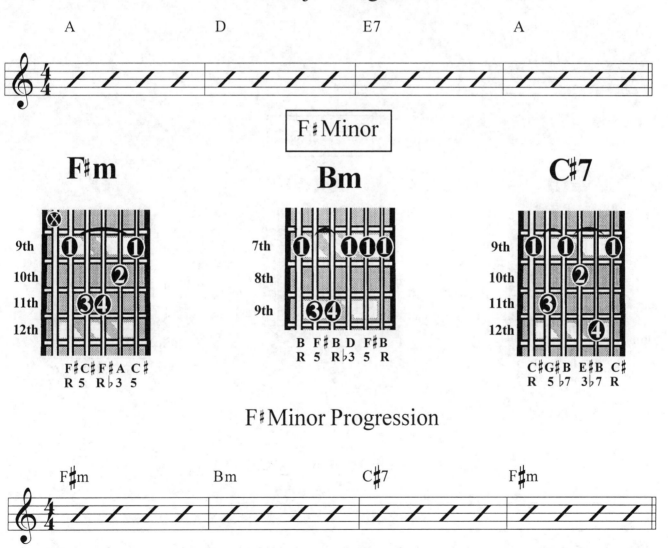

A   D   E7   A

F♯ Minor

F♯m   **Bm**   **C♯7**

```
F♯ C♯ F♯ A  C♯        B  F♯ B  D  F♯ B        C♯ G♯ B  E♯ B  C♯
R  5  R ♭3 5          R  5  R ♭3 5  R          R  5 ♭7  3 ♭7  R
```

F♯ Minor Progression

F♯m   Bm   C♯7   F♯m

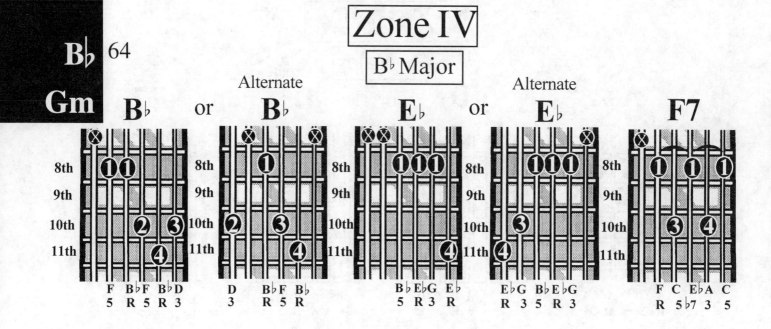

Zone IV
B♭ Major

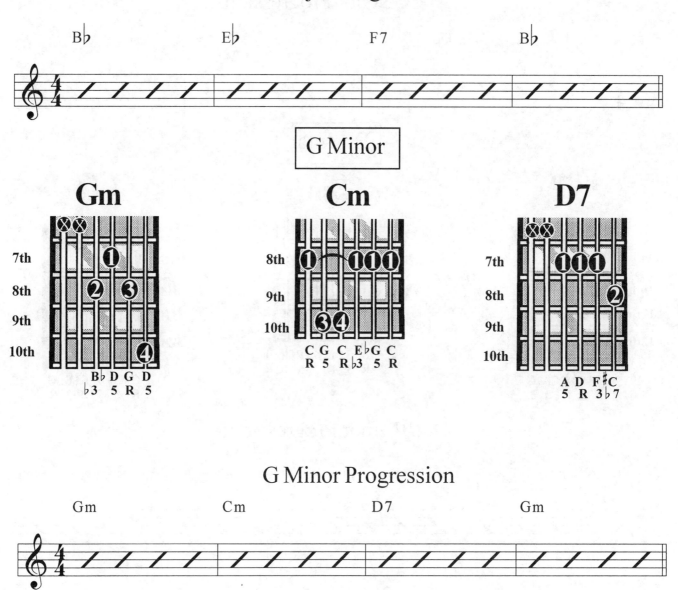

B♭ Major Progression

B♭   E♭   F 7   B♭

G Minor

G Minor Progression

Gm   Cm   D 7   Gm

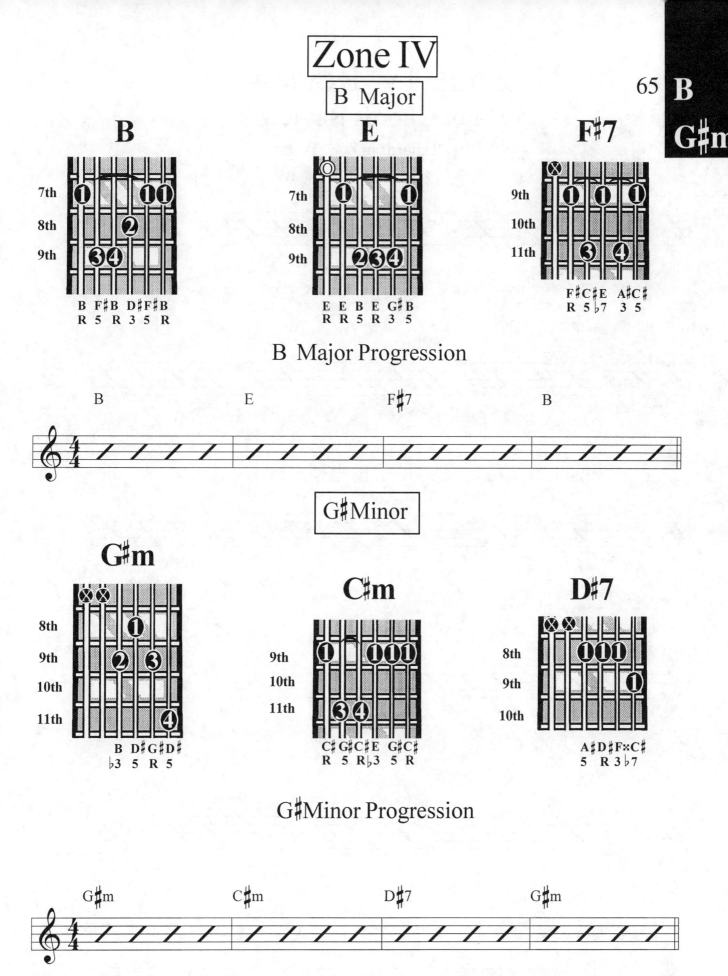

Zone IV

B Major

B Major Progression

G♯ Minor

G♯Minor Progression

IV

Zone IV Review
Major Chords Review
* Play all chords in Zone IV *

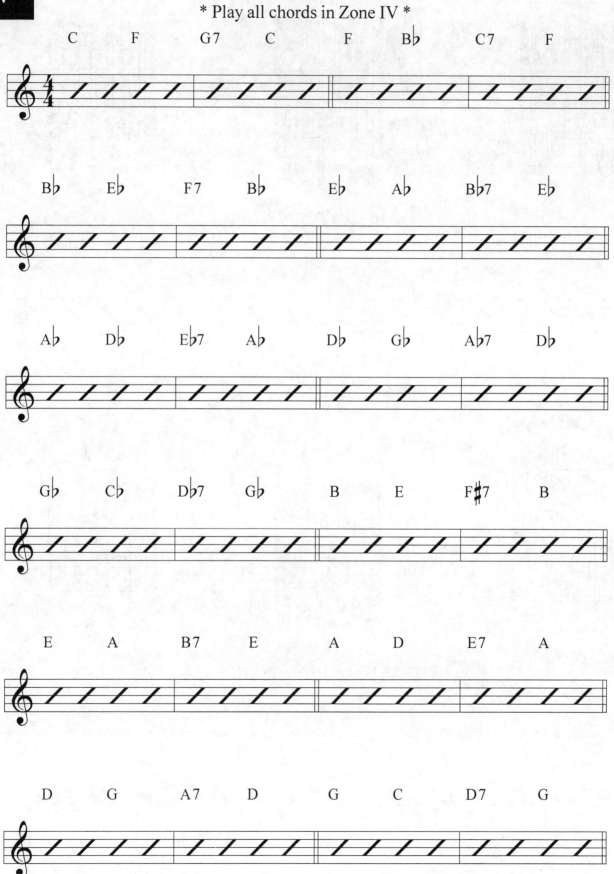

Minor Chords Review

Major/Minor Review

Play Very Slowly

C Am F Dm   G G7 C   F Dm B♭ Gm   C C7 F

B♭ Gm E♭ Cm   F F7 B♭   E♭ Cm A♭ Fm   B♭ B♭7 E♭

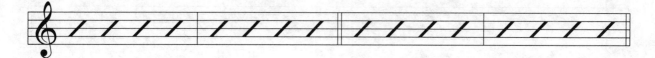

A♭ Fm D♭ B♭m   E♭ E♭7 A♭   D♭ B♭m G♭ E♭m   A♭ A♭7 D♭

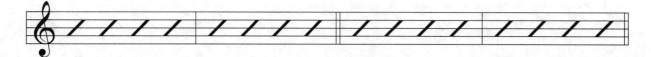

G♭ E♭m B A♭m   D♭ D♭7 G♭   B G♯m E C♯m   F♯ F♯7 B

E C♯m A F♯m   B B7 E   A F♯m D Bm   E E7 A

D Bm G Em   A A7 D   G Em C Am   D D7 G

Zone V

In Zone V the 1st Finger of the Left Hand
will always be between the Ninth and Eleventh Frets.

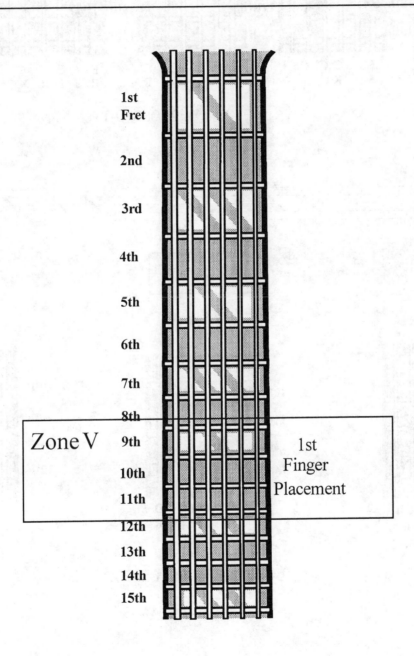

1st
Fret

2nd

3rd

4th

5th

6th

7th

8th

Zone V 9th   1st
                   Finger
10th   Placement

11th

12th

13th

14th

15th

Am

Zone V

C Major

C or Alternate C   F or Alternate F   G7

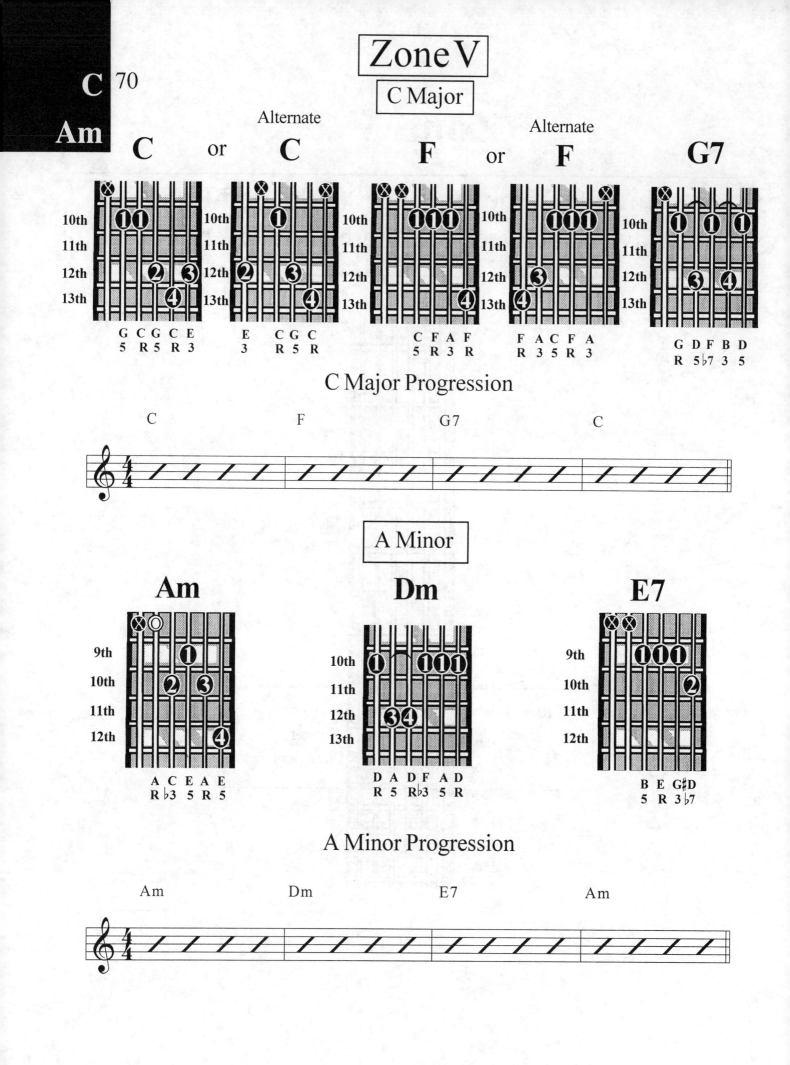

C Major Progression

A Minor

Am   Dm   E7

A Minor Progression

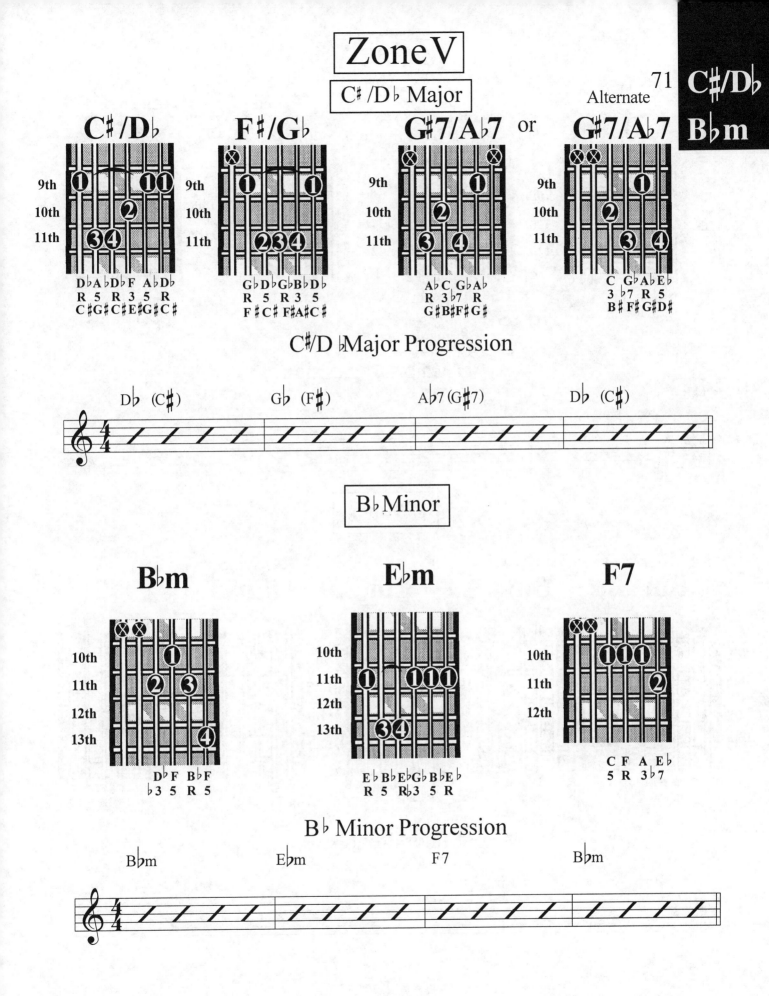

Zone V

C#/Db Major

Bb Minor

C#/Db Major Progression

Bb Minor Progression

Bm

Zone V
D Major

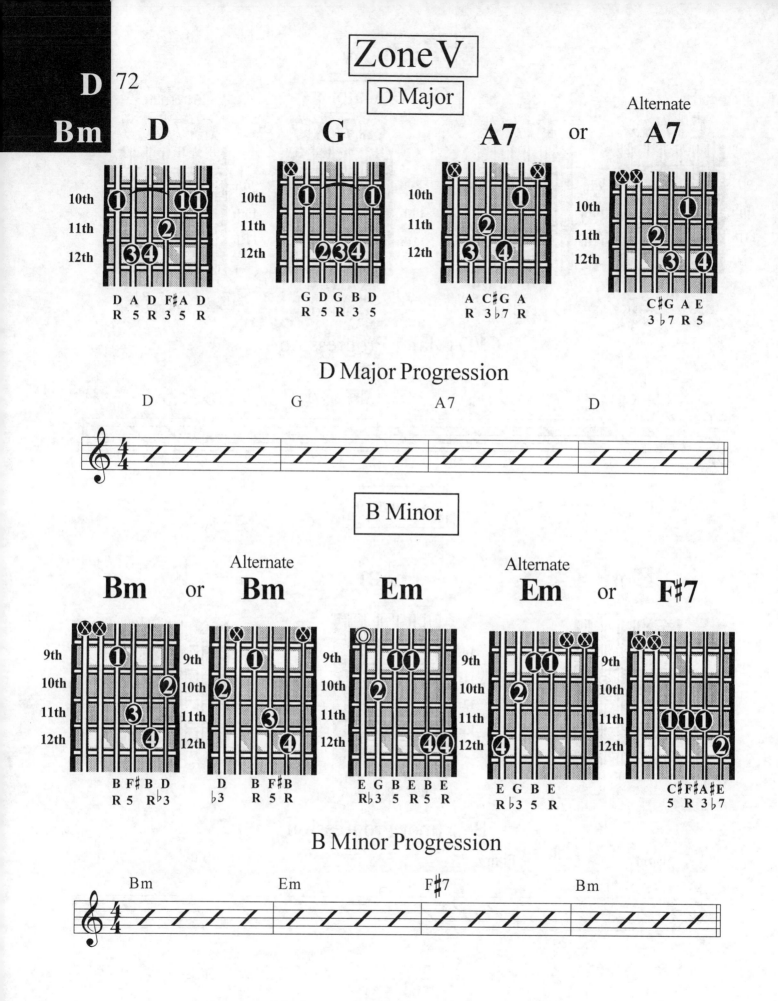

D Major Progression

B Minor

B Minor Progression

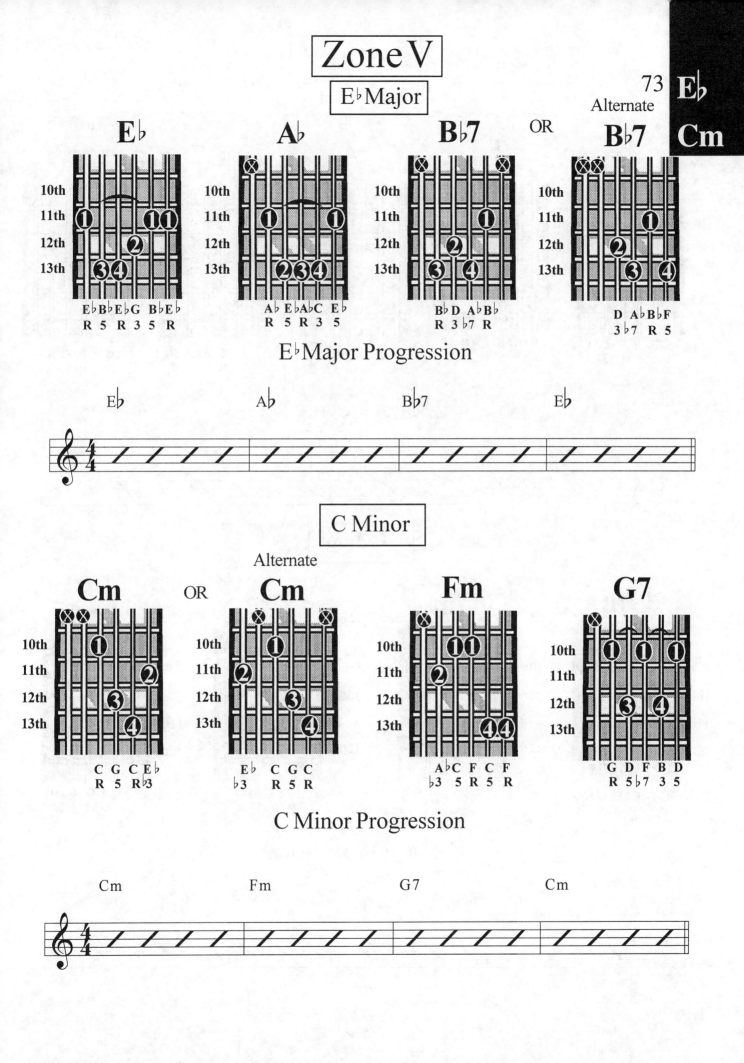

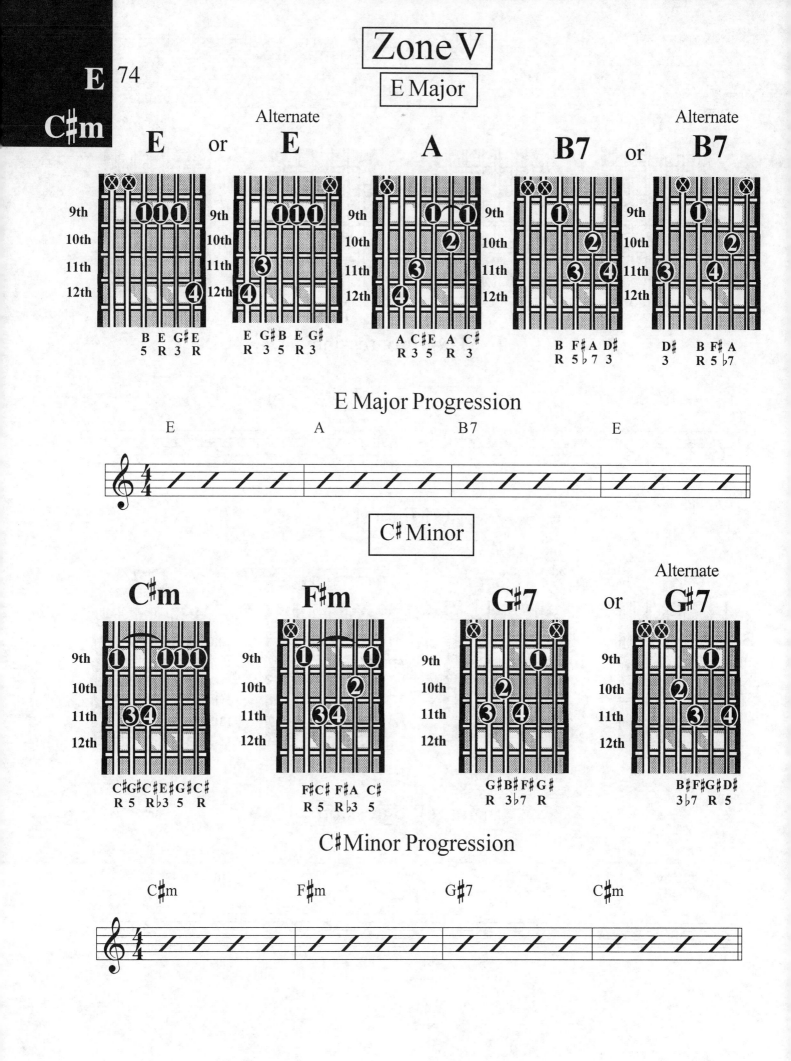

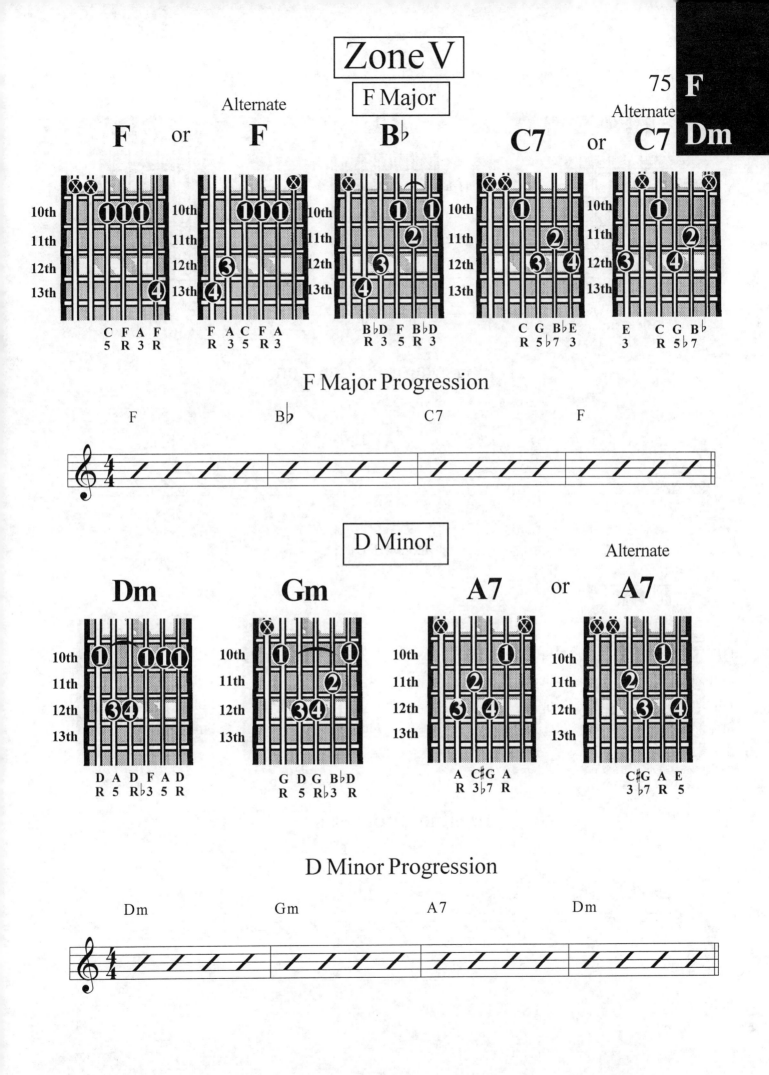

Zone V
F♯/G♭ Major

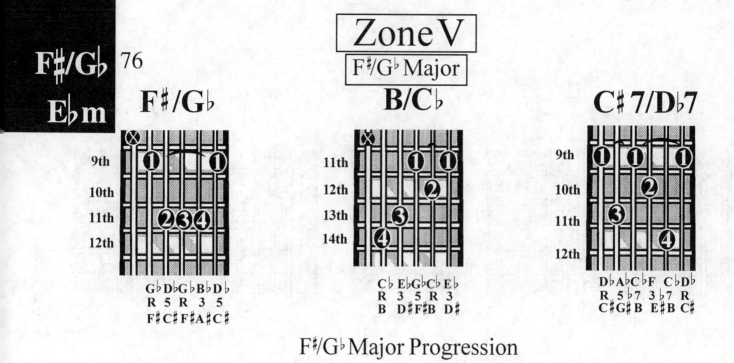

F♯/G♭

9th
10th
11th
12th

G♭D♭G♭B♭D♭
R 5 R 3 5
F♯C♯F♯A♯C♯

B/C♭

11th
12th
13th
14th

C♭ E♭G♭C♭ E♭
R 3 5 R 3
B D♯F♯B D♯

C♯7/D♭7

9th
10th
11th
12th

D♭A♭C♭F C♭D♭
R 5 ♭7 3 ♭7 R
C♯G♯B E♯B C♯

F♯/G♭ Major Progression

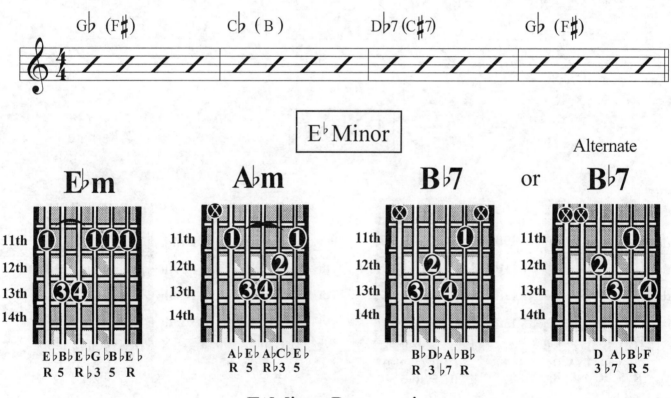

G♭ (F♯)   C♭ (B)   D♭7 (C♯7)   G♭ (F♯)

E♭ Minor

E♭m

11th
12th
13th
14th

E♭B♭E♭G♭B♭E♭
R 5 R♭3 5 R

A♭m

11th
12th
13th
14th

A♭E♭A♭C♭E♭
R 5 R♭3 5

B♭7

11th
12th
13th
14th

B♭D♭A♭B♭
R 3 ♭7 R

Alternate
B♭7

11th
12th
13th
14th

D A♭B♭F
3 ♭7 R 5

E♭ Minor Progression

E♭m   A♭m   B♭7   E♭m

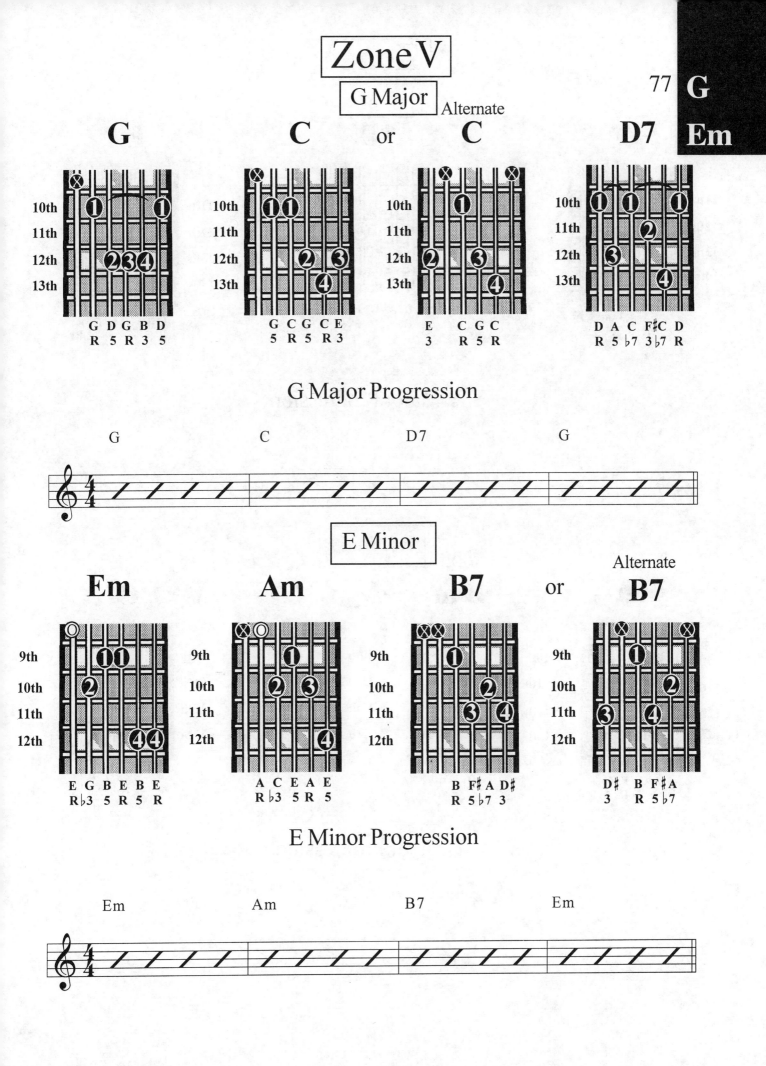

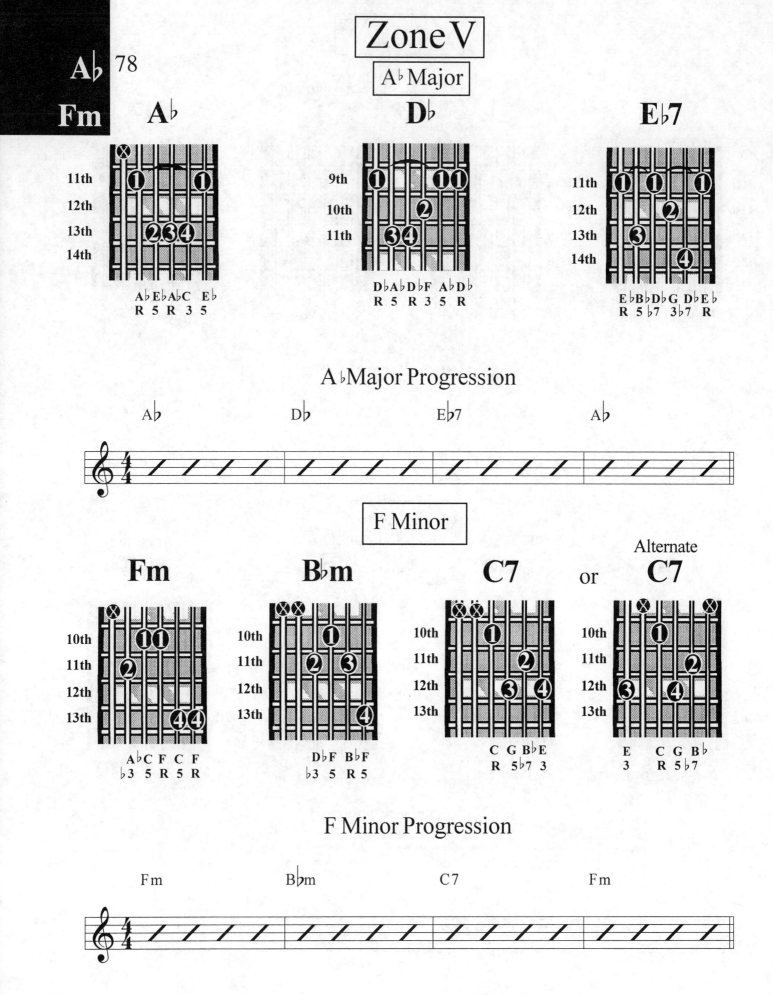

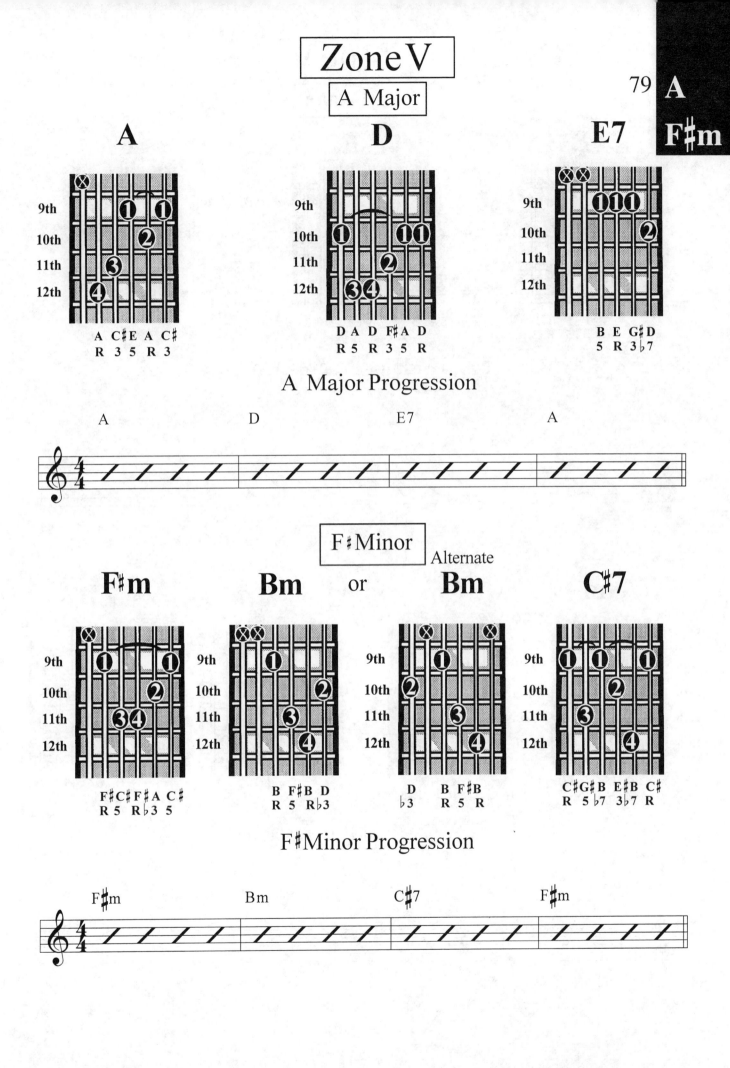

Zone V

A Major

A

9th
10th
11th
12th

A C#E A C#
R 3 5 R 3

D

9th
10th
11th
12th

D A D F#A D
R 5 R 3 5 R

E7

9th
10th
11th
12th

B E G#D
5 R 3♭7

A Major Progression

A   D   E7   A

F# Minor

Alternate

F#m

9th
10th
11th
12th

F#C#F#A C#
R 5 R♭3 5

Bm

9th
10th
11th
12th

B F#B D
R 5 R♭3

or

Bm

9th
10th
11th
12th

D   B F#B
♭3   R 5 R

C#7

9th
10th
11th
12th

C#G#B E#B C#
R 5♭7 3♭7 R

F#Minor Progression

F#m   Bm   C#7   F#m

Zone V

B♭ Major

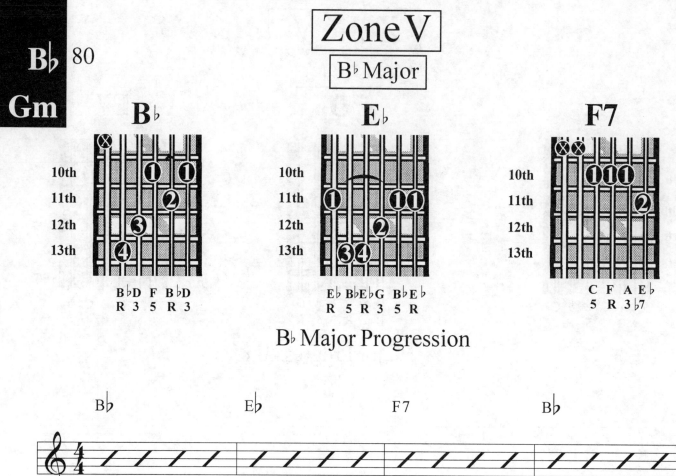

B♭ Major Progression

G Minor

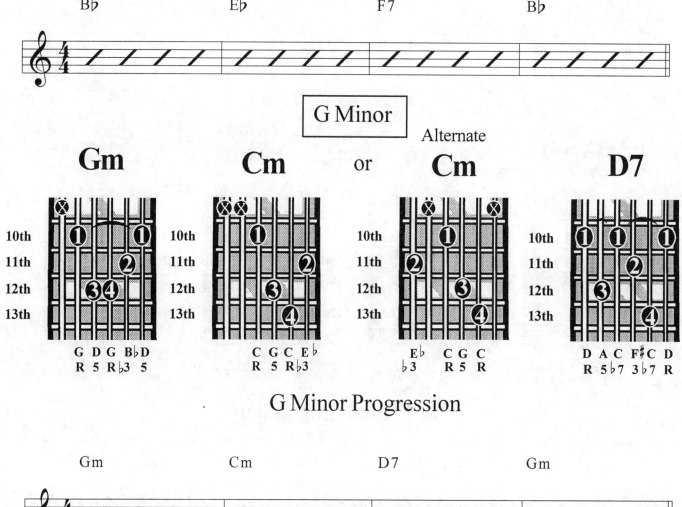

G Minor Progression

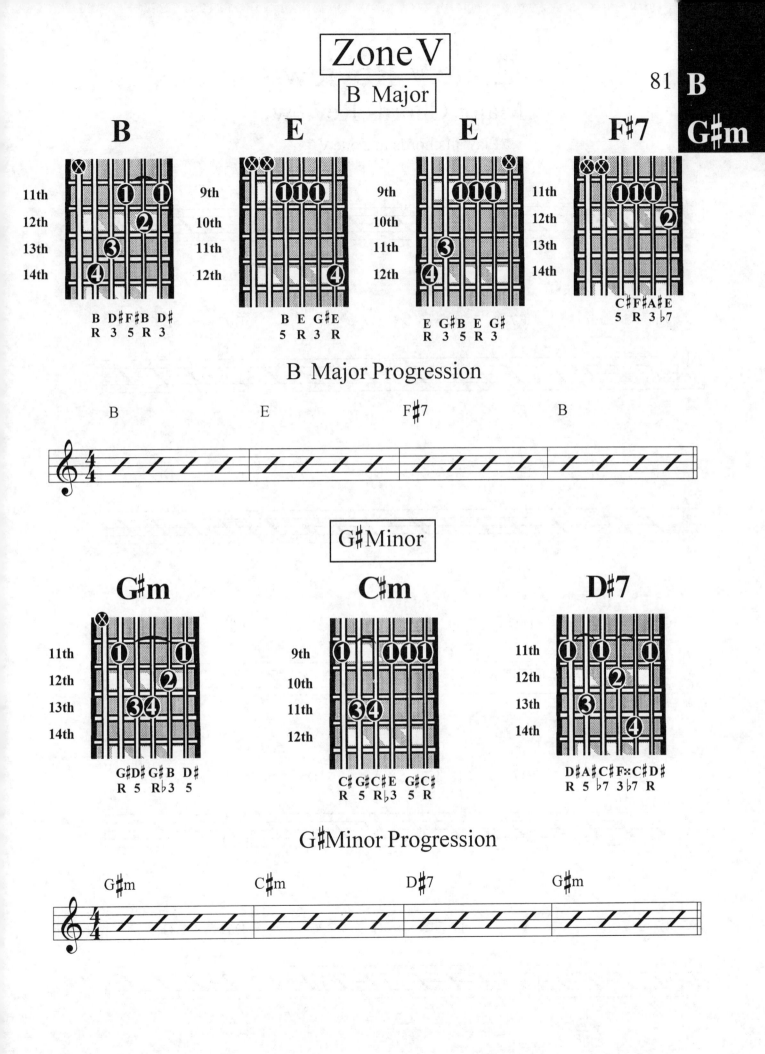

Zone V Review
Major Chords Review
* Play all chords in Zone V *

C   F   G7   C   F   B♭   C7   F

B♭   E♭   F7   B♭   E♭   A♭   B♭7   E♭

A♭   D♭   E♭7   A♭   D♭   G♭   A♭7   D♭

G♭   C♭   D♭7   G♭   B   E   F♯7   B

E   A   B7   E   A   D   E7   A

D   G   A7   D   G   C   D7   G

Minor Chords Review

Major/Minor Review

Play Very Slowly

C Am F Dm   G G7 C   F Dm B♭ Gm   C C7 F

B♭ Gm E♭ Cm   F F7 B♭   E♭ Cm A♭ Fm   B♭ B♭7 E♭

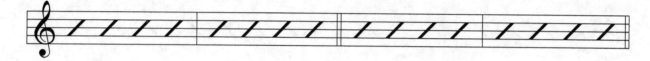

A♭ Fm D♭ B♭m   E♭ E♭7 A♭   D♭ B♭m G♭ E♭m   A♭ A♭7 D♭

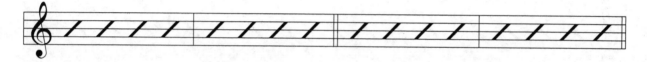

G♭ E♭m B A♭m   D♭ D♭7 G♭   B G♯m E C♯m   F♯ F♯7 B

E C♯m A F♯m   B B7 E   A F♯m D Bm   E E7 A

D Bm G Em   A A7 D   G Em C Am   D D7 G

Appendix:

Music Theory & Additional Chords

Basic Music Alphabet

The Basic Music Alphabet has only 7 Letters.

They are: A - B - C - D - E - F - G - (A) ⟵ Back to our first letter

If you start with any of the letters and continue, the pattern repeats itself.

B - C - D - E - F - G - A - (B)

C - D - E - F - G - A - B - (C)

D - E - F - G - A - B - C - (D)

E - F - G - A - B - C - D - (E)

F - G - A - B - C - D - E - (F)

G - A - B - C - D - E - F - (G)

Whole Steps - Half Steps

In the Musical Alphabet the distance between some notes (or Alphabet letters) is what we call a ***whole step***. The distance between some others is less and so we call this a ***half step***.

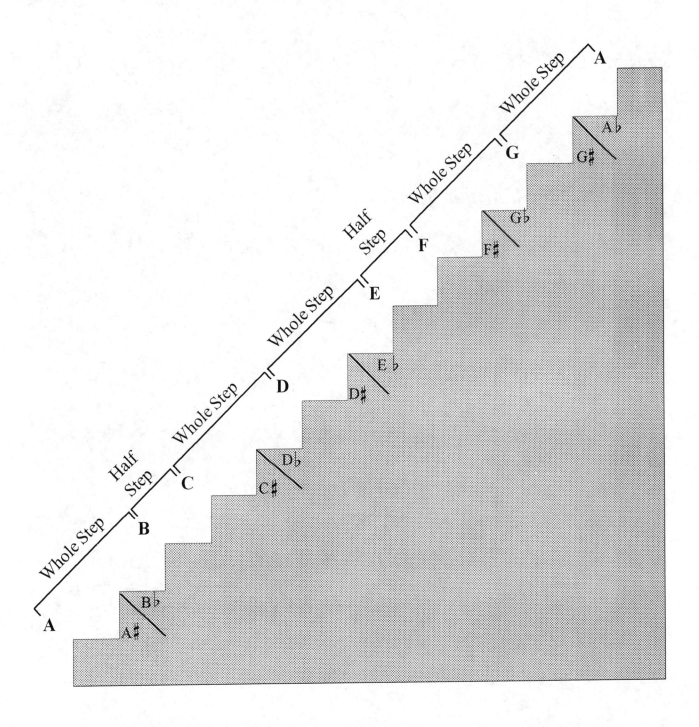

C Scale

Let us start with the letter C and climb the stairs.

This is the *C Major Scale*

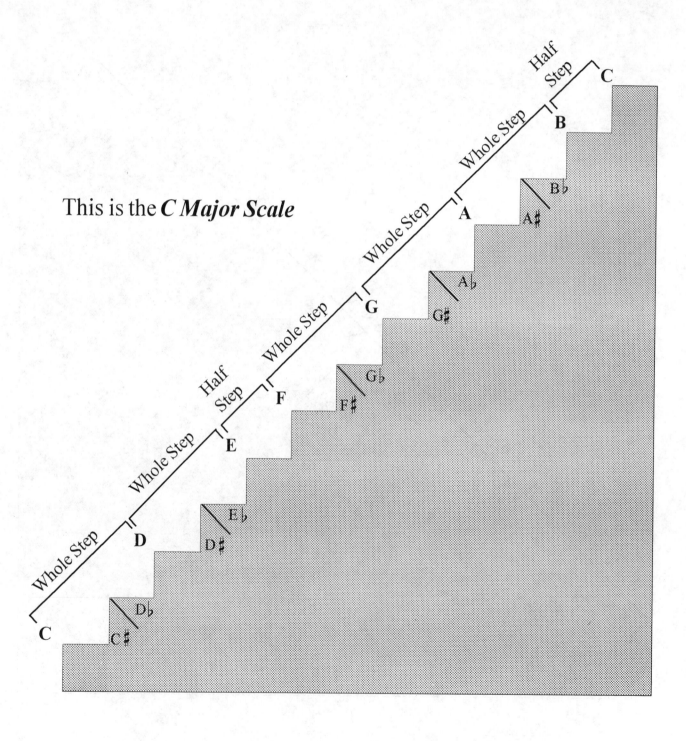

Major Scale Formula

We can now see the Formula for constructing any major scale.

Beginning note called *Root* or *Tonic*

Example: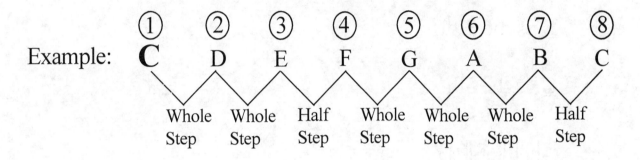

Thus, to build a *Major Scale* we have this Formula.

① Root or Tonic

② Whole Step

③ Whole Step

④ Half Step

⑤ Whole Step

⑥ Whole Step

⑦ Whole Step

⑧ Half Step

Major Chords

A Major Chord has the 1st, 3rd, and 5th Tones of a Scale. Thus, in the key of C, the notes in a C Major Chord are: C - E - G.

C is the Root or Tonic

E is the 3rd

G is the 5th

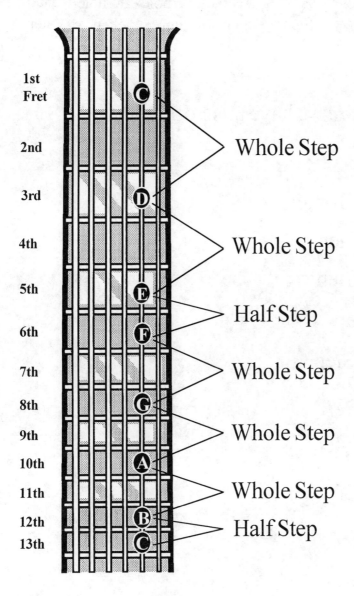

Major Keys / Major Scales

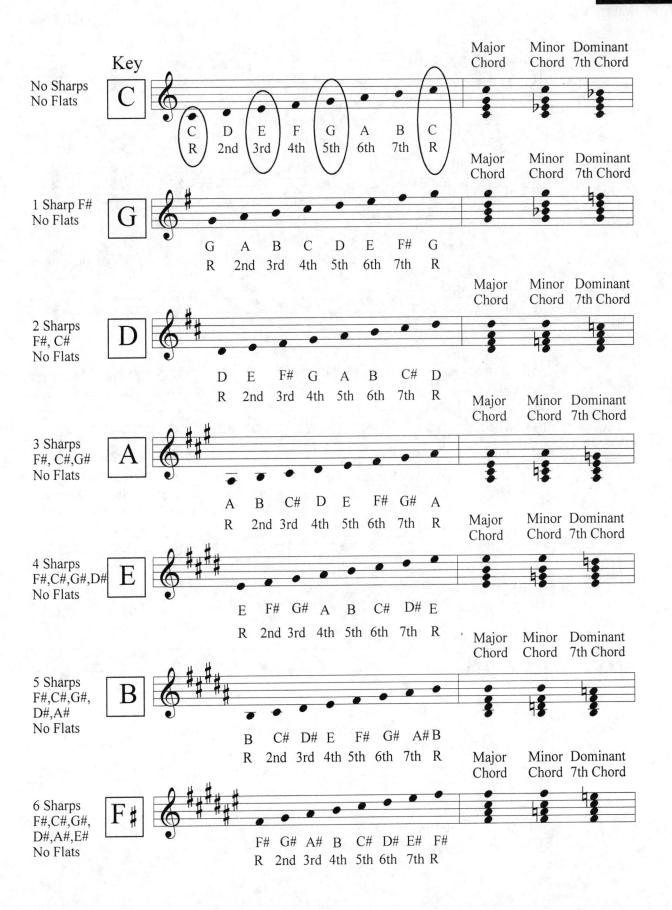

Major Keys / Major Scales

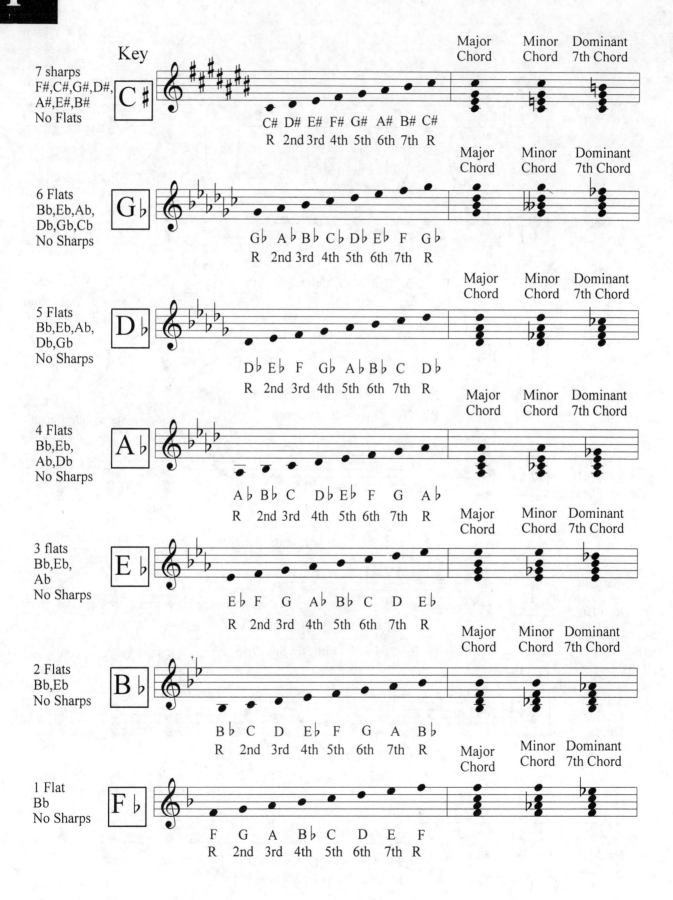

Chord Building Chart*

Chord Type	Scale Degrees Used	Symbols
Major	Root, 3rd, 5th	Maj
Minor	Root, ♭3rd, 5th	mi, -, m
Diminished	Root, ♭3rd, ♭5th, ♭♭7th	dim, °
Augmented	Root, 3rd, ♯5th	+, aug.
Dominant Seventh	Root, 3rd, 5th, ♭7th	dom 7,7
Minor Seventh	Root, ♭3rd, 5th, ♭7th	-7, min7
Major Seventh	Root, 3rd, 5th, Maj. 7th	M7, ma7, △, 7̄
Major Sixth	Root, 3rd, 5th, 6th	M6, 6
Minor Sixth	Root, ♭3rd, 5th, 6th	mi 6,-6
Seventh ♯5th	Root, 3rd, ♯5th, ♭7th	7^{+5}, $7^{♯5}$
Seventh ♭5th	Root, 3rd, ♭5th, ♭7th	7^{-5}, $7^{♭5}$
Major 7th♭3rd	Root, ♭3rd, 5th, maj. 7th	Ma 7^{-3}
Minor 7th, ♭5th	Root, ♭3rd, ♭5th, ♭7th	Mi 7^{-5}, $-7^{♭5}$
Seventh Suspended 4th	Root, 4th 5th, ♭7th	7 sus 4, 7 sus
Ninth	Root, 3rd, 5th, ♭7th, 9th	9
Minor Ninth	Root, ♭3rd, 5th, ♭7th, 9th	mi 9,- 9
Major Ninth	Root, 3rd, 5th, maj. 7th, 9th	Ma 9
Ninth Augmented 5th	Root, 3rd, ♯5th, ♭7th, 9th	9^{+5}, $9^{♯5}$
Ninth Flatted 5th	Root, 3rd, ♭5th, ♭7th, 9th	9^{-5}, $9^{♭5}$

*Note- To arrive at scale degrees above 1 octave, (i.e. 9th, 11th, 13th) continue your scale up 2 octaves and keep numbering. The 2nd scale degree will be the 9th tone as you begin your second octave.

I

Chord Building Chart

Chord Type	Scale Degrees Used	Symbols
Seventh ♭9	Root, 3rd, 5th, ♭7th, ♭9th	7^{-9} , $7^{♭9}$
Augmented Ninth	Root. 3rd, 5th, ♭7th, ♯9th	9^+ , 7^{+9}
9/6	Root, 3rd,5th, 6th, 9th	$\frac{9}{6}$, 6 add 9
Eleventh	Root, 3rd, 5th,♭7th, 9th, 11th	11
Augmented Eleventh	Root, 3rd, 5th, ♭7th, 9th, ♯11th	11+, 7 aug 11
Thirteenth	Root, 3rd, 5th, ♭7th, 9th, 11th, 13th	13
Thirteenth♭9	Root, 3rd, 5th,♭7th,♭9th, 11th, 13th	$13^{♭9}$
Thirteenth♭9♭5	Root, 3rd,♭5th, ♭7th,♭9th, 11th, 13th	$13^{♭9♭5}$
Half Diminished	Root, ♭3rd, ♭5th, ♭7th	$\varnothing$

KEY	MAJOR	MINOR	AUG.	DIM	DOM 7th
Key of C Major No ♯'s - No ♭'s	CEG	CE♭G	CEG♯	CE♭G♭B♭♭	CEGB♭
Key of G Major F♯	GBD	GB♭D	GBD♯	GB♭D♭F♭	GBDF
Key of D Major F♯- C♯	DF♯A	DFA	DF♯A♯	DFA♭C♭	DF♯AC
Key of A Major F♯- C♯- G♯	AC♯E	ACE	AC♯F	ACE♭G♭	AC♯EG
Key of E Major F♯- C♯- G♯- D♯	EG♯B	EGB	EG♯C	EGB♭D♭	EG♯BD
Key of B Major F♯- C♯- G♯- D♯- A♯	BD♯F♯	BDF♯	BD♯F×	BDFA♭	BD♯F♯A
Key of F♯ Major F♯- C♯- G♯- D♯- A♯- E♯	F♯A♯C♯	F♯AC♯	F♯A♯C×	F♯ACE♭	F♯A♯C♯E
Key of C♯ Major F♯- C♯- G♯- D♯- A♯- E♯- B♯	C♯E♯G♯	C♯EG♯	C♯E♯G×	C♯EGA♯	C♯E♯G♯B
Key of F Major B♭	FAC	FA♭C	FAC♯	FA♭C♭D	FACE♭
Key of B♭ Major B♭- E♭	B♭DF	B♭D♭F	B♭DF♯	B♭D♭F♭G	B♭DFA♭
Key of E♭ Major B♭- E♭- A♭	E♭GB♭	E♭G♭B♭	E♭GB	E♭G♭B♭♭	E♭GB♭D♭
Key of A♭ Major B♭- E♭- A♭- D♭	A♭CE♭	A♭C♭E♭	A♭CE	A♭C♭E♭♭F	A♭CE♭G♭
Key of D♭ Major B♭- E♭- A♭- D♭- G♭	D♭FA♭	D♭F♭A♭	D♭FA	D♭F♭A♭♭B♭	D♭FA♭B
Key of G♭ Major B♭- E♭- A♭- D♭- G♭- C♭	G♭B♭D♭	G♭B♭♭D♭	G♭B♭D	G♭B♭♭D♭♭E♭	G♭B♭D♭F♭
Key of C♭ Major B♭- E♭- A♭- D♭- G♭- C♭- F♭	C♭E♭G♭	C♭E♭♭G♭	C♭E♭G	C♭E♭♭FA♭	C♭E♭G♭B♭♭

Chord Reference Chart

KEY	MAJ. 7th	MIN. 7th	MAJ. 6th	MIN. 6th
Key of C Major No ♯'s - No ♭'s	CEGB	CE♭GB♭	CEGA	CE♭GA
Key of G Major F ♯	GBDF♯	GB♭DF	GBDE	GB♭DE
Key of D Major F ♯- C ♯	DF♯AC♯	DFAC	DF♯AB	DFAB
Key of A Major F ♯- C ♯- G ♯	AC♯EG♯	ACEG	AC♯EF♯	ACEF♯
Key of E Major F ♯- C ♯- G ♯-D ♯	EG♯BD♯	EGBD	EG♯BC♯	EGBC♯
Key of B Major F ♯- C ♯- G ♯- D ♯- A ♯	BD♯F♯A♯	BDF♯A	BD♯F♯G♯	BDF♯G♯
Key of F ♯ Major F ♯-C ♯-G ♯-D ♯-A ♯- E ♯	F♯A♯C♯E♯	F♯AC♯E	F♯A♯C♯D♯	F♯AC♯D♯
Key of C ♯ Major F ♯-C ♯-G ♯- D ♯-A ♯ -B ♯	C♯E♯G♯B♯	C♯EG♯B	C♯E♯G♯A♯	C♯EG♯A♯
Key of F Major B ♭	FACE	FA♭CE♭	FACD	FA♭CD
Key of B♭ Major B ♭- E ♭	B♭DFA	B♭D♭FA♭	B♭DF G	B♭D♭FG
Key of E♭ Major B ♭- E ♭ -A ♭	E♭GB♭D	E♭G♭B♭D♭	E♭GB♭C	E♭G♭B♭C
Key of A♭ Major B ♭- E ♭-A ♭- D ♭	A♭CE♭G	A♭C♭E♭G♭	A♭CE♭ F	A♭C♭E♭F
Key of D♭ Major B ♭- E ♭-A ♭-D ♭-G ♭	D♭FA♭C	D♭F♭A♭C♭	D♭FA♭B♭	D♭F♭A♭B♭
Key of G♭ Major B ♭- E ♭-A ♭-D ♭- G ♭- C ♭	G♭B♭D♭F	G♭B♭♭D♭F♭	G♭B♭D♭E♭	G♭B♭♭D♭E♭
Key of C♭ Major B ♭- E ♭-A ♭-D ♭- G ♭-C ♭-F ♭	C♭E♭G♭B♭	C♭E♭♭G♭B♭♭	C♭E♭G♭A♭	C♭E♭♭G♭A♭

Appendix II

Additional Chord Forms

Additional Chord Forms

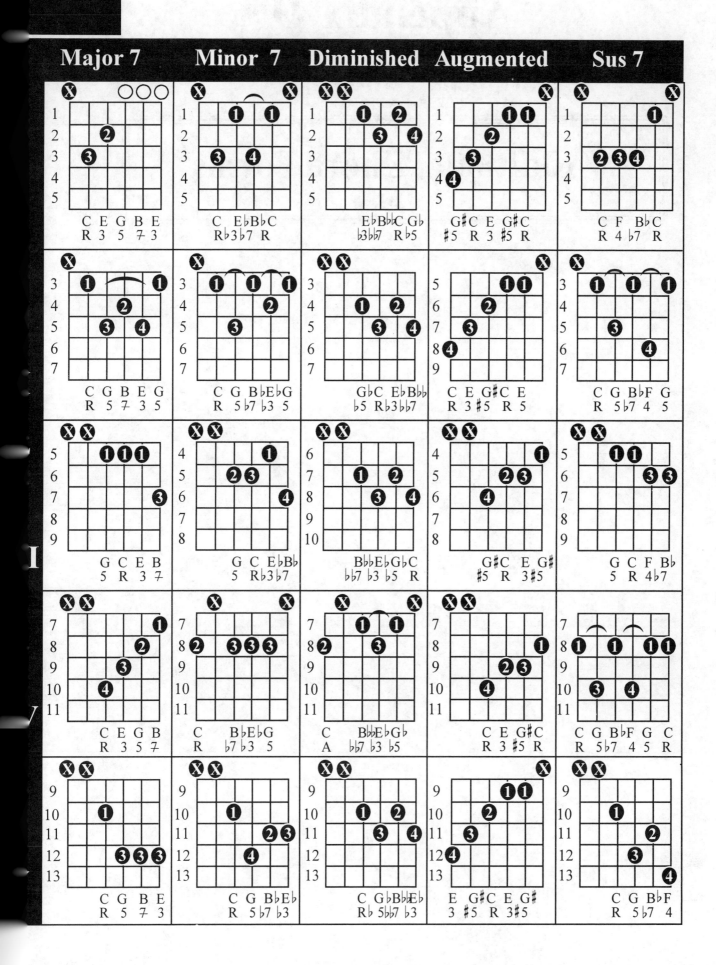

	Major 7	Minor 7	Diminished	Augmented	Sus 7
Zone I	C#E#G#B#E# R 3 5 7 3 Db F Ab C F	C# E B C# R b3 b7 R Db Fb Cb Db	G E BbC# b5 b3b7 R Abb Fb CbbDb	G✗C# E# G✗C# #5 R 3 #5 R A D F A D	C# F B C# R 4 b7 R Db Gb Cb Db
Zone II	C# G# B#E#G# R 5 7 3 5 Db Ab C F Ab	C# G# B E C# R 5 b7 b3 R Db Ab Cb Fb Db	G C#E Bb b5 R b3 b7 AbbDb F Cb	G✗ C#E# G✗ #5 R 3 #5 A Db F A	C# G# B F#G# R 5 b7 4 5 Db Ab Cb Gb Ab
Zone III	G#C#E#B# 5 R 3 7 AbDbF C	G#C#E B 5 R b3 b7 Ab Db Fb Cb	Bb G C#E bb7 b5 R b3 Cbb AbbDbFb	C#E G✗C#E R 3 #5 R 3 DbF A Db F	G#C#F#B 5 R 4 b7 Ab DbGbCb
Zone IV	C#E#G#B# R 3 5 7 Db F Ab C	C# B E G# R b7 b3 5 Db Cb Fb Ab	C# Bb E G R bb7 b3 b5 Db CbbFb Abb	C# E# G✗C# R 3 #5 R Db F A Db	C#G# B F#G#C# R 5 b7 4 5 R DbAb Cb GbAbDb
Zone V	C#E#G#B#E# R 3 5 7 3 Db Ab C F	C# G#B E R 5 b7 b3 Db Ab Cb F	C# G Bb E R b5 bb7 b3 Db Abb CbbF	E#G✗C#E#G✗ 3 #5 R 3 #5 F A DbF A	C# G B F# R 5 b7 4 Db Ab Cb Gb

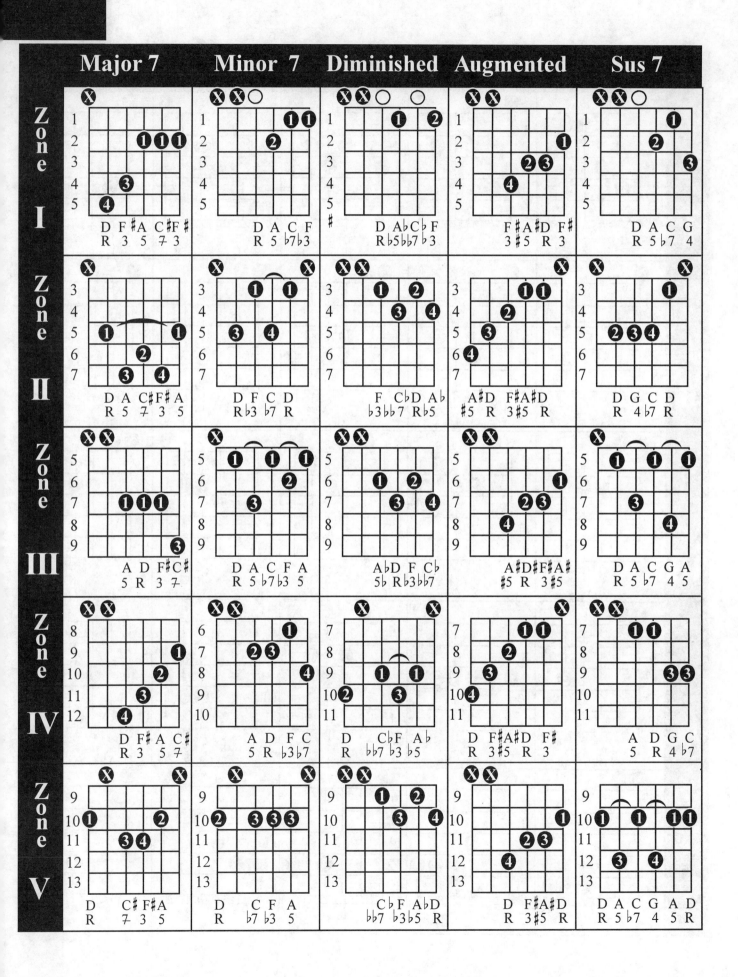

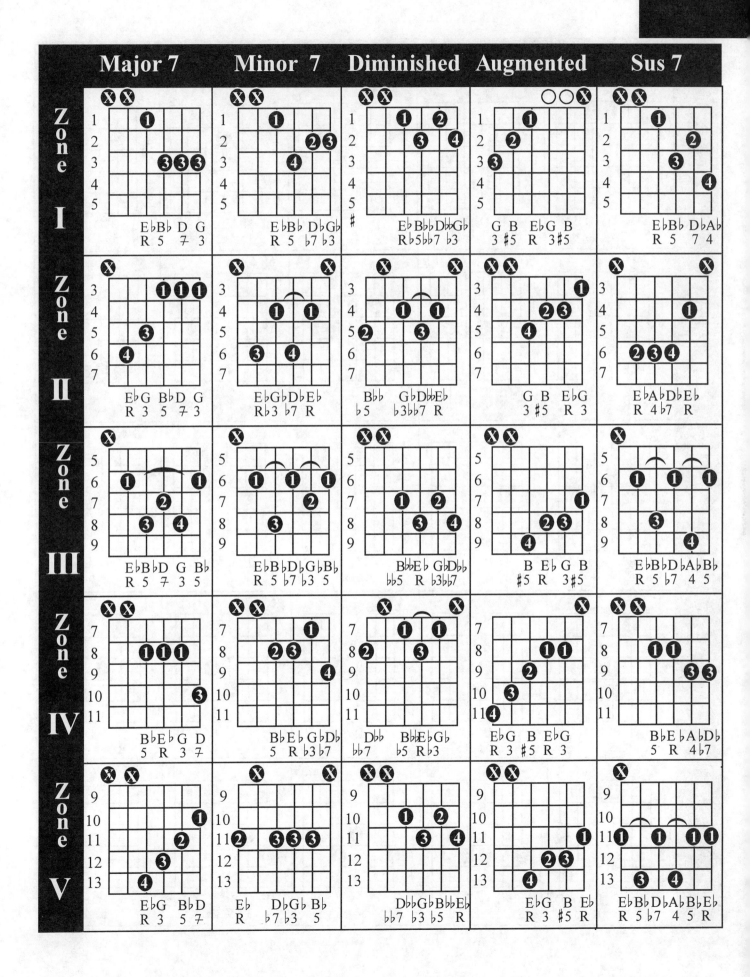

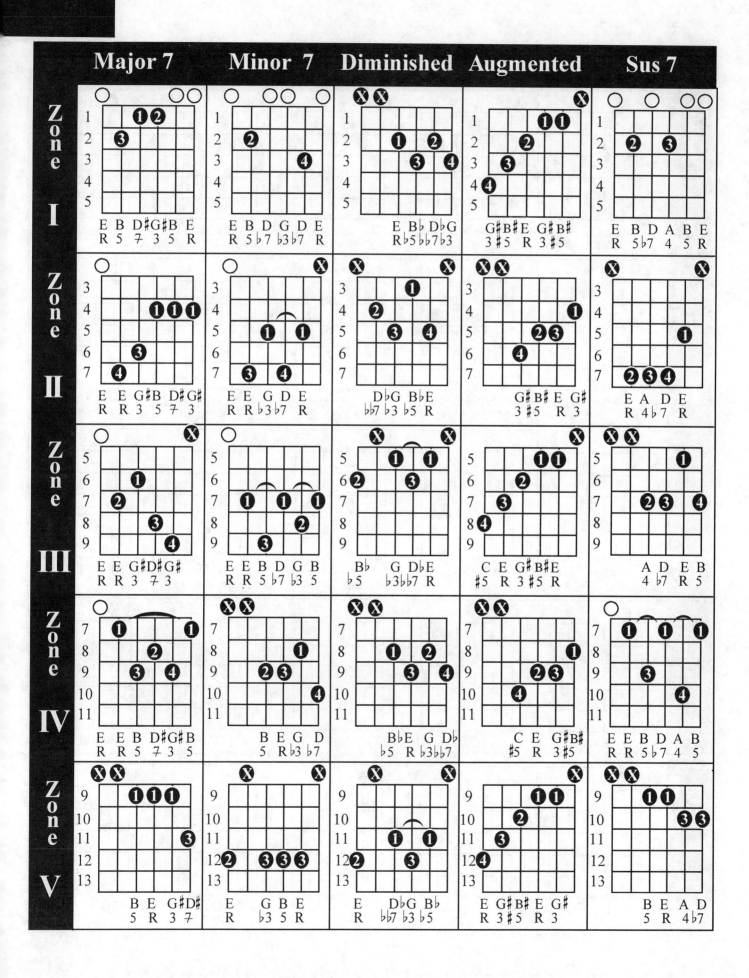

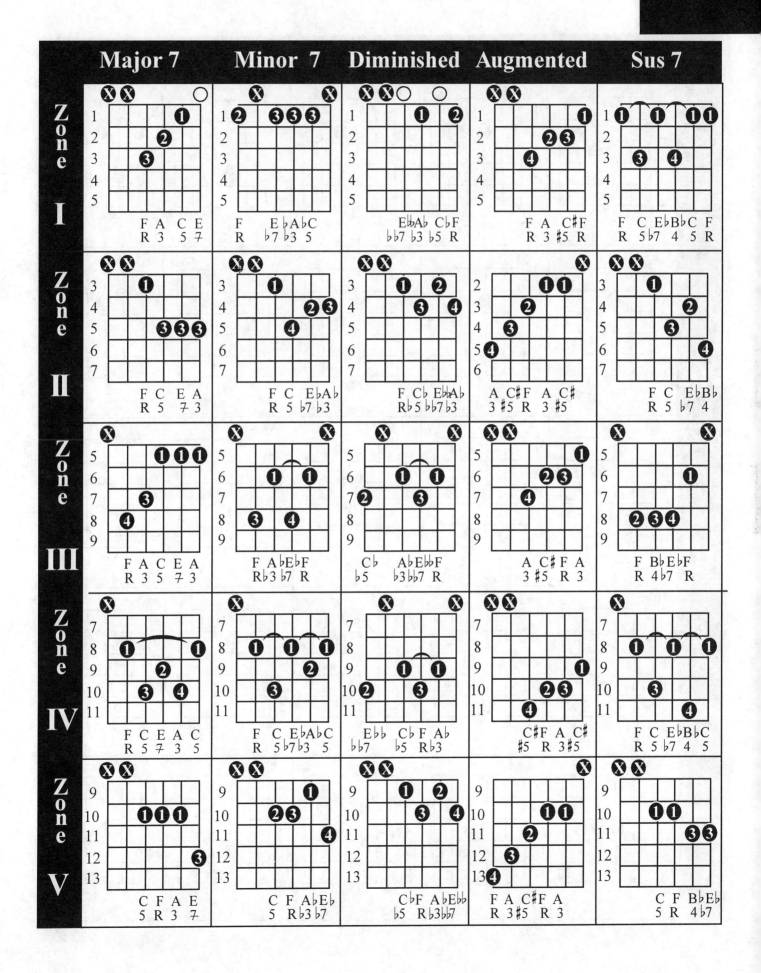

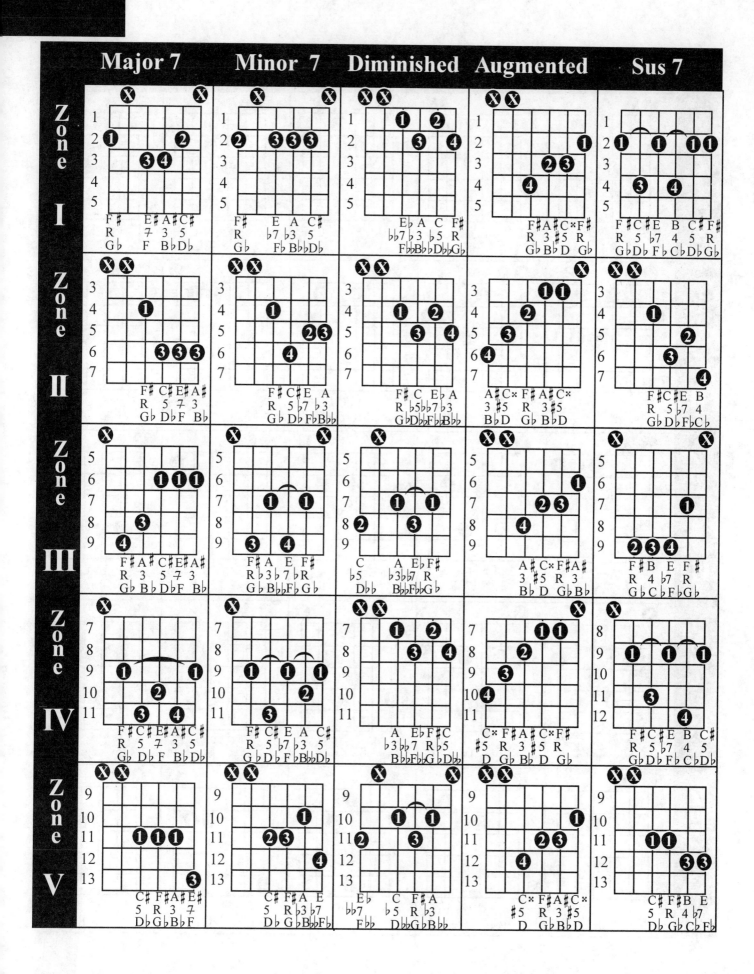

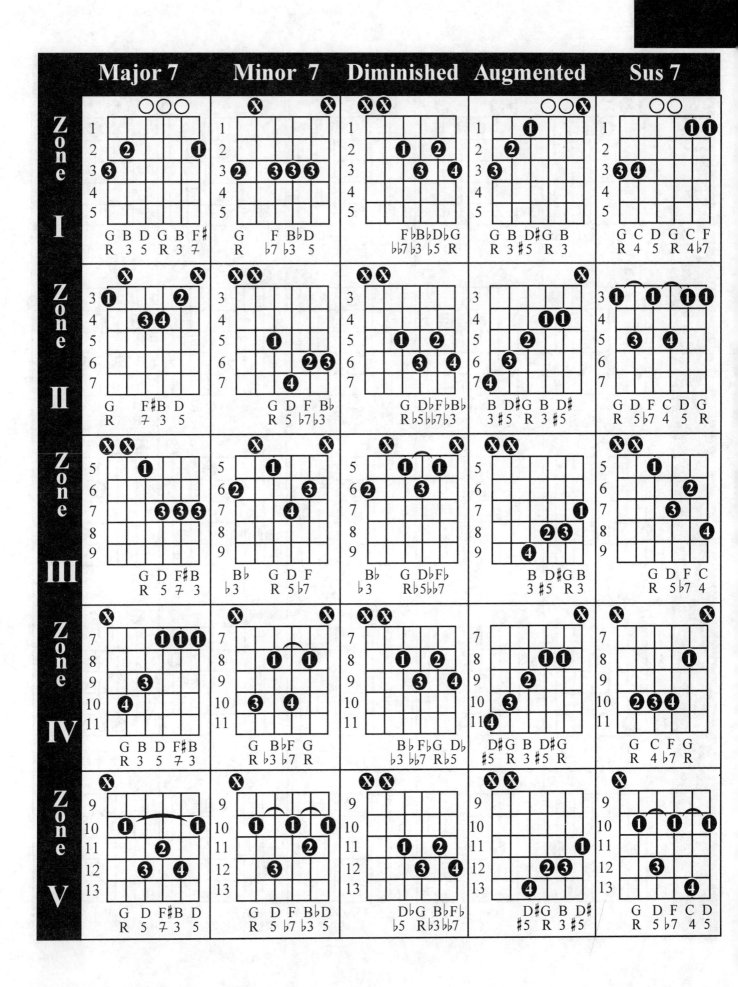

Additional Chord Forms

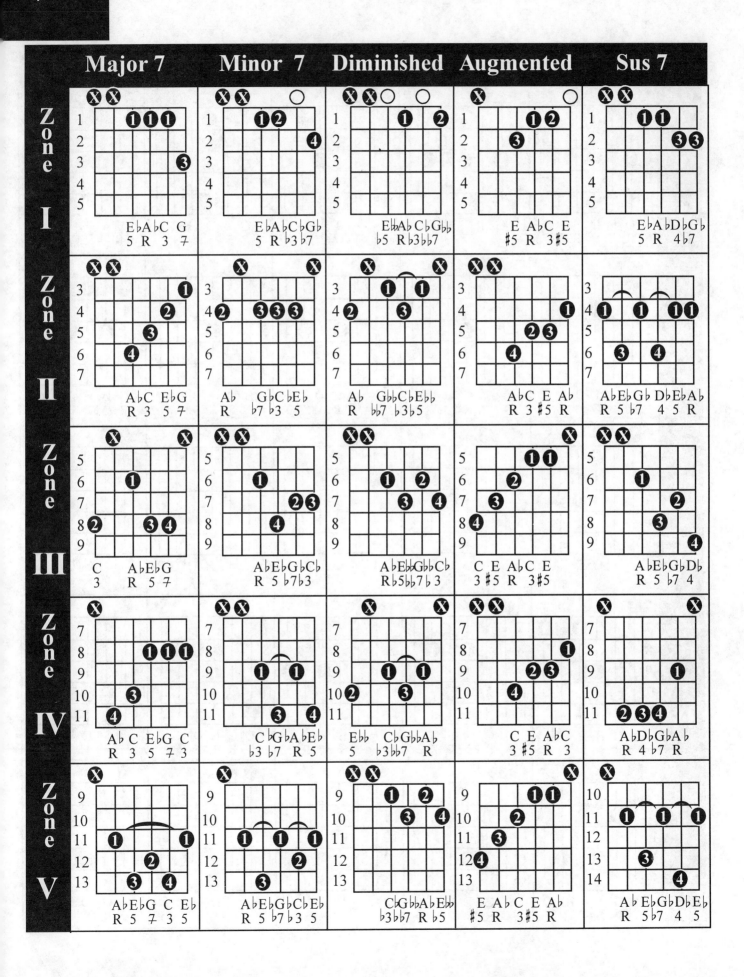

	Major 7	Minor 7	Diminished	Augmented	Sus 7
Zone I	A E G# C# E R 5 7 3 5	A E G C E R 5 b7 b3 5	A Eb A C Gb R b5 R b3 bb7	A E# A C# E# R #5 R 3 #5	A E G D E R 5 b7 4 5
Zone II	A A C# E G# R R 3 5 7	A G C E R b7 b3 5	A Gb C Eb R bb7 b3 b5	A A C# E# A R R 3 #5 R	A E A D G R 5 R 4 b7
Zone III	A G# C# E R 7 3 5	A A E G C R R 5 b7 b3	A A Eb Gb C R R b5 bb7 b3	C# E# A C# E# 3 #5 R 3 #5	A E G D E A R 5 b7 4 5 R
Zone IV	A A E G# C# R R 5 7 3	C A E G b3 R 5 b7	C A Eb Gb b3 R b5 bb7	A C# E# A C# R 3 #5 R 3	A A E G D R R 5 b7 4
Zone V	A C# E G# C# R 3 5 7 3	A C G A R b3 b7 R	A C Gb A Eb R b3 bb7 R b5	E# A C# E# A #5 R 3 #5 R	A D G A R 4 b7 R

Additional Chord Forms

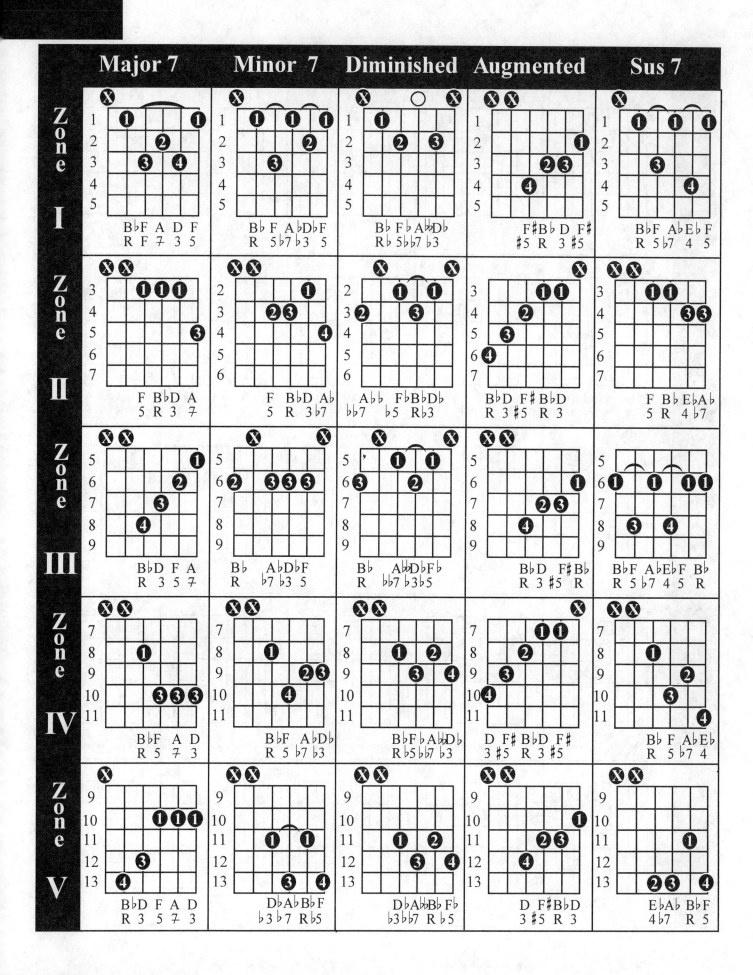